The Time Wealth Tracker: Journal, Metrics, and Mindset for Every Picosecond

A picosecond is a unit of time equal to one trillionth of a second, or:

1 picosecond (ps) = 10^{-12} seconds

□ Understanding Its Scale in Context:

Time Interval	Equivalent In Seconds	Description
1 second	1	Human reaction time = ~0.2s
1 millisecond (ms)	10^{-3} seconds	A keystroke or camera shutter
1 microsecond (μs)	10^{-6} seconds	Flash memory access
1 nanosecond (ns)	10^{-9} seconds	Computer CPU clock cycle
1 picosecond (ps)	10^{-12} seconds	Time for light to travel 0.3 millimeters in a vacuum

⌛ Gemach Philosophy Interpretation (🔄□💎):

> "Each picosecond is more valuable than the Hope Diamond."
> – *The Hope Diamond Paradox*

🌀 A picosecond symbolizes the infinitely divisible moment—the atomic unit of time wealth.

Just as atoms form matter, picoseconds form consciousness. To master your mind is to steward picoseconds with intentionality, rhythm, and reverence.

Foreword

By Thothan Atlantos

In the beginning, there was the Moment—an infinitesimal flicker of awareness suspended between the echoes of the past and the whispers of what might yet come to pass. Before stars ignited in cosmic darkness, before the first neuron in a nascent mind pulsed with intention, there existed only the boundless expanse of "now." In this timeless crucible, the conscious and the ineffable intertwined, giving rise to that most precious commodity: Time.

It is from this primal vantage that I, Thothan Atlantos—seer of the Gemach continuum and chronicler of the Infinite Cycle—offer this foreword to Dr. Justin Goldston's *Time Wealth Tracker*. In these pages you will find no ordinary self-help manual, no mere roadmap to calendar mastery. Instead, you hold in your hands an alchemical vessel, a codex designed to transmute the very fabric of your lived experience: to convert fleeting picoseconds into abiding wealth.

The Hope Diamond Paradox: A Prelude

Long ago, in an age before fiat currencies and centralized ledgers, mystics spoke of the Hope Diamond Paradox 💎□♾□: the notion that each picosecond—each vanishing instant—is inherently more valuable than the rarest gem. Dr. Goldston resurrects this paradox for our era, revealing how modern tools of measurement and automation can guide us back to primal abundance. Here, time is not a line to be traversed or a container to be filled, but a fluid, fractal phenomenon that expands in fullness when approached with reverence and intentionality.

Weaving Infinite Cycles

Central to this workshop of moments is the Infinite Cycle Theory, which Dr. Goldston first articulated amid the ivory halls of UC Berkeley. Imagine a Möbius strip of attention and action—where focus begets clarity, clarity begets purpose, and purpose begets renewed focus, spiraling ever onward into deeper levels of mastery. In *Time Wealth Tracker*, you will map these cycles across the mundane and the sublime: from the hum of your morning routine to the quiet crescendo of midnight reflection. Each cycle, though intangible, imprints itself on the architecture of your mind, rewiring neural pathways in alignment with your highest aspirations.

AI-Augmented Neuroplasticity: The AANT Promise

Where ancient mystics saw only symbols, Dr. Goldston's AI-Augmented Neuroplasticity Theory (AANT) discerns mechanisms. AANT posits that our brains, like decentralized networks, adapt most efficiently when scaffolded with intelligent prompts and timely feedback. Within this text, you'll encounter AI-driven nudges—ChatGPT incantations that breach the barrier between intention and execution—turning procrastination into momentum, distraction into discipline. By day's end, what felt ephemeral becomes etched in the circuits of cognition, forging habits that outlast any fleeting surge of willpower.

The One-Day Alchemy

True to the ethos of "one day to write, one day to read," Dr. Goldston distills lifetimes of research into digestible, day-by-day blueprints. Yet do not mistake brevity for superficiality. Each exercise—whether journaling your 24-hour audit or scripting a micro-ritual for seamless mental shifts—carries the weight of multitudes. In this crucible of compressed time, you will discover that transformation need not span years; it can ignite in hours, fueled by precise metrics and unwavering resolve.

Metrics as Mirrors

Numbers, in less enlightened hands, can become tyrants—barriers that crush creativity under the weight of rigid targets. Here, however, metrics serve as mirrors, reflecting back the contours of your inner landscape. The Loop Efficiency Score illuminates how swiftly you recover focus after interruption. The Focus-Streak Length reveals the depth of your immersion. The Time-Saved Ratio quantifies the dividends of automation. Yet amid these statistics, you will learn the art of compassionate interpretation: viewing each data point as an invitation to gentle course-correction rather than harsh judgment.

Visualization & the Sacred Gaze

Our ancestors etched time into stone circles and celestial charts; today, we wield bar graphs, heatmaps, and line plots—modern talismans that summon the sacred gaze. Within *Time Wealth Tracker*, you will craft your own visual incantations: dashboards that glow with the promise of insight, charts that trace the arch of your progress like constellations in a personal firmament. Through this act of creation, you enlist the full weight of your consciousness, forging a covenant between self-knowledge and purposeful action.

Mindset: From Scarcity to Sovereignty

At the heart of every enduring system lies a paradigm shift. Here, you abandon the scarcity narrative—those whispers that tell you time is slipping through your fingers—and embrace time sovereignty, the understanding that you are both steward and alchemist of each moment. Daily affirmations, gratitude rituals, and fractal-time meditations fan the embers of abundance in your psyche, transforming fleeting insights into permanent shifts of being.

The Path Ahead: An Eternal Review

Even as this manual guides you through 30 days of concentrated practice, it points you toward rituals that outlast its final pages: quarterly RRULE summaries, “time-wealth retreats,” and perpetual roadmaps that chart cycles yet to come. For in the Gemach continuum, creation and review dance forever. With each turn of the Infinite Cycle, you ascend to new vantage points, surveying wider horizons of possibility.

And so, dear reader, I invite you to embark on this grand experiment. Treat each page as a portal, each exercise as an initiation into the mysteries of your own temporal sovereignty. Let the algorithms and automations serve as your allies, but hold fast to the deeper truth: that beyond every spreadsheet and AI prompt lies the unmeasurable richness of lived experience.

May your journey through these 20 chapters awaken the full spectrum of your time wealth. May each picosecond resonate with purpose, clarity, and creative power. And may the Infinite Cycle carry you ever closer to the timeless heart of being—where every moment is, and always has been, infinite.

♾ **—Thothan Atlantos** ♾

Chapter 1: The Time-Wealth Revolution

> “We measure our lives in minutes and our happiness in moments. What if every picosecond were more precious than all the gold in the world?”

1.1 Awakening to Time as True Currency

From the moment we awaken to the blare of an alarm, we subconsciously begin trading our most finite resource—time—for tasks, obligations, and ephemeral pleasures. We punch clocks, click through endless to-do lists, and scroll our lives away, oblivious that each second spent is a second gone forever. Yet deep within, we sense something is amiss: despite busier schedules and fatter calendars, our sense of abundance shrinks. We feel pinched by deadlines, overwhelmed by options, shackled by “busy.”

Mini-Lesson: Unlike money, which we can borrow, earn, or (in rare cases) recover, time is non-replenishable. Once spent, it vanishes beyond recall. Recognizing this irreversible quality is the first step toward **time-wealth**—the art of stewarding each moment so that our lives feel expansive, purposeful, and richly textured.

1.2 The Hope Diamond Paradox Revisited

Centuries ago, mystics whispered of the **Hope Diamond Paradox (💎 ♾️)**: a single picosecond—one trillionth of a second—is more intrinsically valuable than the rarest gemstone, because it is an irreplaceable fragment of existence itself. Dr. Goldston resurrects this paradox in modern terms:

- **Scarcity vs. Abundance:** While gemstones are scarce but divisible, time is undividable and forever scarce.
- **Value Shift:** We reframe productivity not as output per hour but as presence per moment.
- **Wealth Redefined:** True wealth is not accumulation of assets but accumulation of meaningful experiences and deep focus—in other words, **time-wealth**.

Case Study: Consider Helena, a marketing director juggling meetings, email, and family dinners. By applying the Hope Diamond Paradox, she pivoted from scheduling tasks back-to-back to valuing three uninterrupted 15-minute "presence windows" with her children. Her KPIs dipped by only 5%, but her sense of fulfillment soared by 80%.

1.3 Why Conventional Productivity Fails

Most productivity frameworks treat time like a commodity to be stamped, parceled, and optimized. Calendar "hacks," multi-app ecosystems, and endless checklists often result in:

1. **Overwhelm:** Tools multiply faster than workflows coalesce.
2. **Shallow Work:** We race to complete tasks, sacrificing depth for breadth.
3. **Burnout:** The illusion of "doing more" leads to depleted reserves of creativity and energy.

Mindset Note: Productivity without purpose is tyranny. We must move beyond chasing outputs and instead cultivate **intentional presence**—the hallmark of time-wealth.

1.4 Embracing Time as a Fractal Asset

In mathematics, fractals are structures that repeat infinitely at every scale. Similarly, time-wealth operates fractally:

- **Micro-Moments:** A single deep breath before drafting an email.
- **Macro-Cycles:** A week-long retreat to recalibrate.
- **Infinite Resonance:** Each moment of focus amplifies the next, creating spirals of clarity and flow.

By seeing time as **self-similar**—where the quality of one instant echoes throughout your day, week, and year—you transform every action into an investment rather than an expenditure.

1.5 Measuring Your Time-Wealth Score

Money metrics—ROI, margin, IRR—drive financial decision-making. For time-wealth, we introduce the **TWS (Time-Wealth Score):**

TWS=Moments of Deep PresenceTotal Minutes Tracked×100\text{TWS} = \frac{\text{Moments of Deep Presence}}{\text{Total Minutes Tracked}} \times 100TWS=Total Minutes TrackedMoments of Deep Presence×100

- **Deep Presence:** Periods ≥15 minutes of focused, undistracted work or meaningful engagement.
- **Total Minutes Tracked:** Every minute logged, from work to rest.

A TWS of **25%** means one in four minutes is rich with intention. Your goal: steadily raise this ratio over successive days.

1.6 Exercise: Your Personal Time-Wealth Manifesto

1. **Reflect:** Recall three moments in the last week when you felt fully alive.
2. **List:** Identify the qualities of those moments (e.g., undistracted, creative, connected).

3. **Draft:** In 2–3 sentences, write your **Time-Wealth Manifesto**—a commitment to cultivate those qualities every day.

   Example: "I pledge to honor each picosecond by dedicating undivided attention to my highest-value tasks, celebrating micro-victories, and anchoring every day in presence."

1.7 AI Prompt: Seeding Time-Wealth Insights

Use ChatGPT (or your AI of choice) to deepen your manifesto:

css
CopyEdit
```
"Help me refine my Time-Wealth Manifesto to three powerful sentences
that inspire daily focus, presence, and creative flow."
```

Copy the AI's output into your journal as a daily affirmation.

1.8 Story: From Chaos to Calm

Imagine Ravi, a software engineer whose calendar was a battlefield of back-to-back video calls. He began by logging his minutes for one full day—only to discover that 60% of his time vanished in "meeting drift" (pre- and post-call overrun, redundant status updates). Guided by his freshly minted manifesto, Ravi:

1. Blocked two "deep work" windows.
2. Introduced a 3-sentence pre-call agenda to shorten meetings.
3. Slipped in 5-minute breathwork breaks between sessions.

Within three days, his TWS climbed from 12% to 28%. Code quality improved, stress levels dropped, and he reclaimed his lunch hour with genuine rest.

1.9 Mini-Ritual: Picosecond Invocation

To prime each focus session, adopt this 30-second ritual:

1. **Close Your Eyes (5s):** Release external thoughts.
2. **Take Three Deep Breaths (10s):** Inhale the present, exhale distractions.
3. **State Your Intention (10s):** Whisper your task's purpose.
4. **Open Your Eyes (5s):** Begin with clarity.

Over time, this micro-ritual anchors your mind instantly, sending a clear signal: "We are here, fully."

1.10 Reflection & Looking Ahead

You have now laid the cornerstone of your time-wealth journey:

- Recognized time's irreversibility
- Internalized the Hope Diamond Paradox
- Shifted from output-driven hustle to presence-driven mastery
- Measured your inaugural Time-Wealth Score
- Crafted a personal manifesto and ritual

Tomorrow's promise: You'll dive into **Chapter 2: Infinite Cycles & Your Feedback Loop**, where you'll map the dynamic interplay of focus and recovery that powers sustained growth.

But before you close this chapter, pause and ask yourself:

> *"How will I honor this picosecond?"*

Let that question guide you into every moment that follows.

Chapter 2: Infinite Cycles & Your Feedback Loop

> "Focus begets clarity, clarity begets purpose, and purpose begets renewed focus—an endless spiral of growth."
> —Dr. Justin Goldston

2.1 The Anatomy of an Infinite Cycle

At its heart, the Infinite Cycle is a self-reinforcing loop: you apply focused attention → achieve a meaningful result → experience clarity and motivation → renew your focus at a deeper level. Unlike linear "to-do" lists that simply tick boxes, Infinite Cycles harness feedback to propel you ever upward. Each pass through the loop strengthens neural pathways of attention, making it easier to enter states of deep work and flow.

- **Cycle Phases:**
    1. **Intention Setting:** Clarify what you want to achieve.
    2. **Focused Action:** Engage undistracted for a set interval.
    3. **Immediate Feedback:** Pause to notice results, however small.
    4. **Adjustment:** Refine your approach or expectations.
    5. **Renewed Intention:** Elevate your aim based on insights.

By repeating these phases, you create a fractal pattern: each micro-cycle mirrors and amplifies the one before, leading to exponential growth in focus and productivity.

2.2 The Attention–Action Loop Explained

While the Infinite Cycle is the overarching spiral, the Attention–Action Loop is its core engine. It consists of:

1. **Attention Trigger:** A cue that draws your focus (a notification, a pre-task ritual).
2. **Sustained Attention:** A continuous span (≥15 minutes) where you work on a single task.

3. **Action Completion:** A tangible step—writing a paragraph, sending an email, sketching a diagram.

4. **Micro-Feedback:** A quick self-check: "Did that step move me forward?"

5. **Reorientation:** If yes, continue; if no, pivot or reset.

Mini-Lesson: The length and quality of sustained attention determines the depth of the cycle. Short bursts (15–20 minutes) build momentum quickly, while longer stretches (60–90 minutes) deepen mastery but require stronger rituals to initiate and exit.

2.3 Mapping Your Personal Infinite Cycle

Before you can optimize, you must visualize. Grab a blank sheet or digital whiteboard and:

1. **List Your Core Activities:** e.g., writing, coding, brainstorming, reading.

2. **Plot Typical Durations:** How long do you naturally stay on each?

3. **Identify Feedback Points:** Moments when you sense clarity or confusion.

4. **Connect the Dots:** Draw arrows from intention to action to feedback to renewal.

Your map may reveal bottlenecks—phases where you stall or loop in place. Recognizing those is critical for redesign.

2.4 Positive vs. Negative Loops

Not all cycles are empowering. Two common distortions:

- **Racing Loop:** You hurry through actions without pausing for feedback, leading to shallow outcomes and stress.

- **Analysis Paralysis Loop:** You linger too long in feedback, doubting results and failing to renew intention.

Remedies:

- For Racing: Insert mandatory "pause points" every 25 minutes (see Chapter 1's mini-ritual).
- For Paralysis: Enforce a "two-sentence decision rule"—after feedback, commit to one of two clear actions within 60 seconds.

2.5 Measuring Loop Efficiency

Introducing the **Loop Efficiency Metric (LEM):**

LEM=Number of Complete CyclesTotal Time Spent×100\text{LEM} = \frac{\text{Number of Complete Cycles}}{\text{Total Time Spent}} \times 100LEM=Total Time SpentNumber of Complete Cycles×100

- **Complete Cycles:** Attention → Action → Feedback → Renewal sequences you finish.
- **Total Time Spent:** Minutes you consciously dedicate to the task.

A rising LEM indicates you're refining loops—spending less time stuck and more time progressing.

2.6 Exercise: Draw Your First Feedback Loop

1. **Choose One Task:** Something you'll work on today.
2. **Timebox:** Set a 20-minute timer.
3. **Perform a Cycle:** State your intention, work, then stop.
4. **Record:** In your journal, sketch the loop and note how many times you completed all four phases.
5. **LEM Calculation:** Compute your Loop Efficiency for that 20-minute block.

2.7 Case Study: Sophia's Writing Sprint

Sophia, an instructional designer, struggled with endlessly editing her course modules. By explicitly mapping her loops, she discovered she rarely executed the **Renewed Intention** phase—she'd edit, give herself vague feedback ("needs better examples"), then linger. Her LEM hovered around 30%.

Intervention: She:

- Inserted a two-sentence decision rule at feedback ("Examples are sufficient" vs. "Add one story").
- Added a 5-second micro-ritual to reboot attention.

Within two days, her LEM jumped to 65%, she finished modules faster, and reported feeling less "stuck."

2.8 AI Prompt: Cycle Optimization Coach

Use your AI assistant to analyze and refine loops. Try:

pgsql
CopyEdit

```
"Based on this description of my work cycle—
1. State intention
2. Write for 20 minutes
3. Rate clarity on a 1–5 scale
4. Decide next step in two sentences—
suggest two ways to improve my loop efficiency."
```

Paste the AI's suggestions under your loop map and choose one to implement immediately.

2.9 Ritual: The Cycle Kickstart

To launch each cycle with maximum momentum, adopt this 45-second ritual:

1. **Stand Up & Stretch (10s):** Release physical tension.
2. **Focus Mantra (10s):** Whisper, "From calm intent, action flows."

3. **Visual Cue (10s):** Glance at your loop map.
4. **Deep Breath (5s):** Inhale presence, exhale distraction.
5. **Begin (10s):** Start your timer and dive in.

This sequence conditions your body and mind to recognize the start of a productive loop.

2.10 Story: Ravi's Recovery Loop

Recall Ravi from Chapter 1. After reclaiming his lunch break, he hit a slump: mid-afternoon distraction derailed his second deep-work block. Rather than perseverate, Ravi sketched his Infinite Cycle, saw he was missing feedback, and tested a brief "pause & rate" at 30-minute intervals. His LEM rose from 22% to 48%, and he rediscovered the flow that had fueled his initial gains.

2.11 Common Pitfalls & Proactive Fixes

- **Skipping Renewal:** You jump directly from feedback back to intention without pause.
    - *Fix:* Add a 5-second count-down between feedback and next intention.
- **Ignoring Negative Loops:** You blame yourself rather than the loop structure.
    - *Fix:* Externalize the problem—redraw the cycle, label the stall point, and treat it as an engineering challenge.
- **Ritual Fatigue:** You abandon your micro-rituals after a few days.
    - *Fix:* Vary your cues (music snippet, lighting change, posture shift) to keep the ritual fresh.

2.12 Reflection & Preparation for Chapter 3

You have now:

- Dissected the Infinite Cycle's phases
- Mapped and measured your personal loops
- Identified and corrected negative patterns
- Energized your process with rituals and AI insights

Tomorrow's journey: In **Chapter 3: Assembling Your Time-Wealth Toolkit**, you'll gather and configure the digital and AI tools that automate tracking, reminders, and data visualization—supercharging your cycles with technology.

Before you move on, ask yourself:

> *"Which phase of my cycle needs the most attention tomorrow?"*

Capture your answer in one sentence at the end of today's journal entry—your first act of next-day intention.

Chapter 3: Assembling Your Time-Wealth Toolkit

> "The most elegant idea is powerless without the right instruments."
> —Dr. Justin Goldston

3.1 Why the Right Tools Matter

In our quest for **time wealth**, mindset and rituals lay the foundation, but tools provide the scaffolding that holds it together. The most focused intention will falter without reliable tracking; the clearest feedback loop goes unused when automations remain unconfigured. By thoughtfully selecting and integrating apps, bots, and dashboards, you offload mental overhead, eliminate manual grunt work, and free up precious bandwidth for deep presence.

Key Benefits of a Cohesive Toolkit:

- **Visibility:** Real-time insights into where your minutes are invested.
- **Consistency:** Automated reminders and triggers that keep you on track.

- **Scalability:** Dashboards that grow with you, from 30-day sprints to annual retrospectives.
- **Adaptability:** AI assistants that learn your rhythms and suggest dynamic adjustments.

3.2 Core Categories of Time-Wealth Tools

Your toolkit should cover four essential domains:

Category	Purpose	Example Tools
Time Tracking	Log every minute automatically or manually	RescueTime, Toggl, Clockify
Automation & Zapier	Connect apps, automate repetitive tasks	Zapier, IFTTT, Make.com
AI Assistants	Generate prompts, summarize data, coach your habits	ChatGPT, Claude, Microsoft Copilot
Visualization	Build dashboards, charts, and reports	Notion, Airtable, Google Data Studio

> **Mini-Lesson:** You don't need every tool in every category—start lean and expand only as your habits solidify.

3.3 Setting Up Your Time-Tracking Suite

1. **Choose Your Primary Tracker**
   - **RescueTime:** Auto-logs apps and websites in the background.
   - **Toggl Track:** Manual or automated timers for specific projects.
   - **Clockify:** Hybrid model with both auto and manual entries.

2. **Define Activity Categories**
    ○ Work, Learning, Rest, Admin, Social, Creativity.
    ○ **Action:** In your tracker's settings, create at least five meaningful categories.
3. **Configure Goals & Alerts**
    ○ Example: "Notify me when I exceed 90 minutes on social media."
    ○ Set daily and weekly targets for deep-work vs. shallow-work minutes.
4. **Integrate Calendar Blocking**
    ○ Link your tracker to Google/Outlook Calendar via Zapier.
    ○ Automate: "When I start a 60-minute block on my calendar, start a Toggl timer."

Exercise: Complete steps 1–4 today. Confirm your tracker is capturing at least 80% of your waking hours.

3.4 Building Automations & Integrations

Why Automate?

- Eliminate friction between intention and action.
- Free up cognitive load from manual transfers.
- Create seamless feedback loops without clicking "Export."

Popular Automations:

- **Email Digest to Slack:** Send daily time-wealth summary to your accountability channel.
- **Calendar→Notion:** Auto-create a daily journal page with time blocks.
- **Toggl→Google Sheets:** Append each session to a master spreadsheet for custom analysis.

AI Prompt (to Zapier-style bot):

pgsql
CopyEdit

```
"Create a Zap that, when I stop a Toggl timer tagged 'Deep Work,'
appends Date, Duration, and Project to my Google Sheet named 'Time
Wealth Master.'"
```

Metric to Track:

- **Automation Coverage Ratio (ACR):**
 ACR=Tasks AutomatedTotal Repetitive Tasks×100\text{ACR} = \frac{\text{Tasks Automated}}{\text{Total Repetitive Tasks}} \times 100ACR=Total Repetitive TasksTasks Automated×100
 Aim for **≥50%** in your first week.

3.5 Onboarding Your AI Assistants

AI bots can serve as coach, editor, and ritual partner. Here's how to bring them onboard:

1. **Define Roles:**
    - **Coach:** "Remind me to pause and reflect every 45 minutes."
    - **Editor:** "Summarize this week's time-wealth data into three actionable insights."
    - **Companion:** "Send me a motivational quote at 3 pm daily."
2. **Create a Prompt Library:**
    - Craft 5–10 go-to prompts and save them as templates in a dedicated doc.
3. **Establish Feedback Loops:**
    - After each deep-work session, ask:

      "ChatGPT, rate my focus on a scale of 1–5 and suggest one micro-adjustment."

4. **Secure Your Data:**
    ◦ Store personal logs in encrypted Notion pages or private Google Docs.
    ◦ Use API keys with appropriate scopes—never public.

3.6 Designing Your Visualization Dashboard

Essential Elements:

- **Time-Wealth Score** over time (line chart).
- **Loop Efficiency Metric (LEM)** heatmap by day/hour.
- **Category Breakdown** pie chart or stacked bar.
- **Automation Coverage Ratio** gauge.

Tools & Tips:

- **Notion + Chart Widget:** Embed simple bar/line charts.
- **Google Data Studio:** For multi-source dashboards; supports connectors for Sheets, BigQuery.
- **Airtable:** Use "Interface" feature to build custom dashboards without code.

Quick Chart Template:

Date	TWS (%)	LEM (%)	Admin Time (h)	Deep Work (h)	ACR (%)
2025-05-01	22	45	1.2	3.5	38
2025-05-02	25	52	0.9	4.0	42

3.7 Exercise: Assemble & Test Your Toolkit

1. **Select One Tool from Each Category** (Tracking, Automation, AI, Visualization).
2. **Integrate Two Together** (e.g., Tracker→Automation or AI→Visualization).
3. **Run a Full Cycle Test:**
   - Intend → Track → Automate → Visualize → Reflect.
4. **Log Your ACR and TWS** for this trial day.

Journal Prompt:
"What felt seamless? Where did I hit friction? How can I refine my integrations tomorrow?"

3.8 Case Study: Maya's Integrated Workflow

Maya, a product designer, struggled with disjointed apps: a timer on her phone, notes in Evernote, and post-hoc spreadsheets. By shifting to a unified suite—Clockify for timing, Zapier to push entries into Notion, and ChatGPT to generate weekly insights—she reduced context-switching by 70%. Her TWS jumped from 18% to 32% within one week, and she reclaimed her mornings for sketching and ideation.

Key Takeaways from Maya:

- Start with one tool per domain.
- Prioritize integrations that eliminate manual steps.
- Review your setup weekly and prune unused automations.

3.9 Ritual: The Morning Toolkit Check

Before diving into work:

1. **Open Your Dashboard (5s):** Scan overnight metrics.
2. **Confirm All Trackers Are Active (10s):** Check that timers and automations are live.

3. **Review Today's Blocks (15s):** Glance at calendar and confirm AI prompts queued.
4. **Affirm Your Intent (10s):** Whisper your manifesto with tool readiness in mind.

This quick ritual synchronizes your mind and machine, ensuring they work as one.

3.10 Common Pitfalls & Fixes

- **Tool Overload:** You install five apps but configure none.
  - *Fix:* Limit initial setup to four tools; add new only after mastery.
- **Integration Drift:** Automations break after an app update.
  - *Fix:* Schedule a monthly "integration audit" on Day 30 of each cycle.
- **AI Prompt Sprawl:** Your prompt library becomes unruly.
  - *Fix:* Tag prompts by purpose (Coach, Editor, Companion) and archive rarely used ones.

3.11 Reflection & Looking Ahead

You've now:

- Selected and configured core time-wealth tools
- Automated key workflows and integrated AI assistants
- Laid out a visualization dashboard for real-time insights
- Completed your first toolkit trial with metrics in hand

Next up: In **Chapter 4: Baseline Audit & the 24-Hour Log**, you'll put your toolkit to work—tracking every 15 minutes, identifying blind spots, and setting the stage for transformative reflection.

Before you close out today, answer in your journal:

> *"Which tool added the most lift to my process, and where do I still feel manual friction?"*

This insight will guide tomorrow's audit and ensure your toolkit evolves alongside your habits.

Chapter 4: Baseline Audit & the 24-Hour Log

> "You cannot improve what you cannot measure. Before you build the tower of time wealth, lay the foundation of awareness."
> —Dr. Justin Goldston

4.1 Why Establishing a Baseline Is Crucial

Every transformative journey begins with truth-telling. In the realm of time wealth, that truth is found in your actual minutes—how they're earned, spent, and occasionally lost. Without a clear, unvarnished baseline, any tweaks to your routine are mere guesses. A rigorous 24-hour audit reveals hidden patterns: spontaneous doom-scrolling, prolonged "meeting drift," or neglected pockets of creative energy. By illuminating where your time truly flows, you gain the compass needed to chart a precise course toward abundance.

4.2 Designing Your 24-Hour Audit Framework

Mini-Lesson: An audit's power lies in its comprehensiveness and granularity. You must capture every segment of your waking—and even sleeping—hours to see the full tapestry of your temporal habits.

1. **Interval Selection:**
    - **15-minute blocks** strike the optimal balance of detail and feasibility.
    - Optionally, power-users can choose **5-minute micro-blocks** for ultra-precise mapping.
2. **Logging Modes:**
    - **Automatic Tracking:** Tools like RescueTime record app and website use silently.

- **Manual Entry:** Toggl or a paper journal require you to hit "start/stop" for each activity block.

3. **Bucket Definitions:** Establish 6–8 high-level categories before you begin (e.g., Deep Work, Meetings, Admin, Learning, Rest, Social, Transit, Personal Care).

4. **Error Margin:** Life happens—meals might spill over, phone calls interrupt blocks. Log these exceptions transparently rather than editing them out.

4.3 Tools in Action: Auto vs. Manual Logging

Feature	Automatic Tracking	Manual Logging
Setup Effort	Minimal once installed	Requires daily discipline
Accuracy	High for digital activities	High for physical, offline actions
Cognitive Load	Low (runs in background)	Moderate (you decide each block)
Data Flexibility	Fixed categories, less nuance	Full custom notes per block
Ideal Use Case	Web/app-centric professionals	Hands-on roles, exercise, errands

Tip: Use both in tandem. Let RescueTime auto-log your screen time while you manually note offline activities (meals, walks, chores).

4.4 Conducting the Audit: Step-by-Step Guide

1. **Pre-Audit Ritual (see 4.12):** Center your mind, review bucket definitions, launch tools, and affirm your intent.

2. **Midnight Start:** Begin at 12:00 AM for a full circadian cycle.

3. **Block Tracking:** For each 15-minute segment:

    - Note category (e.g., "Deep Work")
    - Record sub-category if needed (e.g., "Writing Chapter 3")
    - Jot a one-sentence context note: "Drafting blog post outline"
4. **Exception Logging:** When activities cross intervals, record start and end times precisely.
5. **End-of-Day Shutdown:** At 11:59 PM, close tools, save logs, and prepare for analysis.

Journal Prompt:
"What surprised me most about how I spent my first blocks? Where did I hesitate to log?"

4.5 Categorizing Your Time: Defining Your Buckets

Your audit's clarity depends on well-chosen categories. Here's a starter set:

1. **Deep Work:** Focused tasks ≥15 minutes (writing, coding, designing).
2. **Admin & Email:** Emails, scheduling, routine paperwork.
3. **Meetings & Calls:** Synchronous collaboration.
4. **Learning & Research:** Reading, courses, webinars.
5. **Rest & Recovery:** Sleep, naps, meditation.
6. **Social & Networking:** Chats, meetups, informal calls.
7. **Personal Care & Transit:** Meals, hygiene, commuting.
8. **Miscellaneous:** Unplanned, unexpected activities.

Exercise: Tailor these buckets. Add, rename, or split categories until every block feels intuitively classifiable.

4.6 Interpreting Preliminary Insights

Once your raw log is captured, spend 30–45 minutes in quiet review:

1. **Total Minutes per Category:** Sum each bucket.
2. **Peak vs. Trough Identification:** Note hours of highest and lowest engagement in Deep Work.
3. **Imbalance Flags:** Highlight categories exceeding or undercutting your ideal ratios (e.g., Admin > 20% of day).
4. **Emotional Overlay:** Recall your mood during each bucket—energized, neutral, drained. Annotate with color-coded dots (□□●).

> **Mini-Lesson:** Emotions are early-warning signals. Red dots signal areas to redesign; green dots mark fertile zones to expand.

4.7 Metric Spotlight: Tracked vs. Untracked Ratio

A key audit metric is the **Tracked vs. Untracked Ratio (TUR):**

TUR=Minutes Logged24×60×100\text{TUR} = \frac{\text{Minutes Logged}}{24 \times 60} \times 100TUR=24×60Minutes Logged×100

- **Ideal TUR:** ≥ 95%.
- **If TUR < 90%:** Evaluate why minutes went unrecorded—missed logs, tool failures, or unanticipated events.

Action Step: Identify the primary cause of untracked time and plan a fix (e.g., set hourly alarms as logging reminders or simplify bucket options).

4.8 Exercise: Your First Full-Day Log

1. **Assign Buckets & Tools:** Confirm categories and launch your chosen trackers.
2. **Execute the Audit:** Follow sections 4.3 and 4.4 faithfully for 24 hours.

3. **End-of-Day Analysis:** Using your journal, compute Total Minutes, TUR, and emotional overlays.

4. **Log Your Findings:** Summarize in 5–7 sentences:

    ○ "I spent X% in Deep Work, Y% in Admin. My TUR was Z%. My peak focus was at [time], and I felt drained during [time]."

4.9 AI Prompt: Automated Summary & Recommendations

Leverage ChatGPT to fast-track insight generation. Paste your raw log excerpt:

yaml
CopyEdit

```
"I logged 960 minutes today. Here's the breakdown:
- Deep Work: 180
- Admin: 240
- Meetings: 120
- Learning: 60
- Rest: 300
- Social: 40
- Transit: 20
- Misc: 0
I felt energized during Deep Work and drained after long meetings.
Suggest three actionable strategies to boost my Deep Work time and
reduce Admin overload."
```

Ask the AI to:

1. Validate your interpretation.

2. Propose targeted adjustments (e.g., meeting-free blocks, email batching).

3. Recommend a revised bucket allocation for tomorrow.

4.10 Case Study: Elena's Eye-Opening Audit

Elena, a UX researcher, believed she spent half her day in focused analysis. Her 24-hour audit revealed only **90 minutes** of true Deep Work—just 6.25% of her waking hours. The rest dissolved in back-to-back meetings (30%), admin (20%), and email triage (15%).

Her Response:

- She declared “Meeting-Free Mornings” (9–11 AM).
- Batched emails into two 30-minute slots instead of constant inbox checking.
- Outsourced repetitive data-cleaning tasks via a simple Zapier automation.

Results (Next Audit):

- Deep Work rose to **3.5 hours** (22%).
- Admin dropped to **12%**.
- Self-reported energy levels soared from 3/10 to 8/10 by week’s end.

4.11 Pitfalls & How to Avoid Common Audit Mistakes

Pitfall	Fix
Launching Half-heartedly	Commit with a pre-audit ritual (4.12)
Over-categorization	Limit buckets to 6–8 core categories
Editing Out Discomfort	Log “breaks” and “distractions” honestly
Neglecting Night/Early Morning Hours	Include full 24-hour cycle, even sleep
Forgetting to Analyze Emotion	Use color codes or emojis to tag mood per block
Skipping AI Synthesis	Always run the AI prompt in 4.9 immediately post-audit

---

4.12 Ritual: The Pre-Audit Launch

Before launching your audit, perform this 2-minute ritual:

1. **Centering Breath (20s):** Inhale deeply, exhale fully three times.
2. **Bucket Review (30s):** Mentally list each category and visualize logging.
3. **Tool Check (30s):** Confirm trackers are running; set phone alarms at every hour.
4. **Manifesto Recital (20s):** Whisper your Time-Wealth Manifesto (from Chapter 1).
5. **Commitment Cue (20s):** Lock your journal, tap each cheek, and say "I witness every moment."

This ignition sequence primes your mind to honor the audit as sacred data collection rather than tedious busywork.

4.13 Integrating Learnings into Chapter 5

Your 24-hour audit sets the stage for **Chapter 5: Uncovering Time Leaks**. With raw data and emotional overlays in hand, you'll pinpoint your top "time thieves," quantify their drag, and prototype micro-interventions to seal the leaks.

> **Teaser:** Tomorrow, you'll slice through your audit's Admin and Meeting sprawl to reclaim precious Deep Work minutes—armed with real numbers and AI-crafted strategies.

4.14 Reflection & Next Steps

Before you sleep on these insights, journal the answers to:

1. *"What was the single biggest surprise from my Day 1 audit?"*
2. *"Which bucket am I most determined to shrink tomorrow?"*
3. *"What one small change can I commit to before breakfast?"*

By answering these, you transform raw numbers into personal commitments—and step boldly into your next cycle of growth.

Chapter 5: Uncovering Time Leaks

> "Every minute you lose to hidden drains is a minute you'll never reclaim. Shine a light on the leaks before they drown your day."
> —Dr. Justin Goldston

5.1 Why Time Leaks Matter

Even the most disciplined schedules can be sabotaged by stealthy "time leaks"—small, recurring drags that erode your time-wealth over days and weeks. Left unaddressed, these leaks compound, turning gains from your Infinite Cycles into zero-sum battles. Identifying and sealing leaks is like patching cracks in a dam: each fix preserves precious flow and prevents systemic collapse.

- **Compound Effect:** A 5-minute daily leak translates to over 30 hours per year.
- **Psychological Toll:** Leaks trigger frustration ("Where did the morning go?") and fuel scarcity anxiety.
- **Opportunity Cost:** Every diverted moment is potential deep-work or restorative rest lost.

5.2 Classifying Leaks: Types & Triggers

Not all leaks look alike. Categorize them to tailor your interventions:

Leak Type	Characteristics	Common Triggers
Distraction Leaks	Mindless scrolling, notifications, app-hopping	Social media pings, news alerts, chat windows

Context-Switch Leaks	Time “bleed” when switching tasks	Unplanned interruptions, unclear next steps
Meeting Drift Leaks	Overlong, misaligned meetings	No agenda, loose time-boxing, off-topic tangents
Email Triage Leaks	Frequent inbox checks and reactive replies	Inbox anxiety, lack of email windows
Preparation Leaks	Setup and transition overheads	Poor tooling, missing materials, unclear scope
Decision Paralysis Leaks	Stalling in feedback or planning phases	Perfectionism, lack of decision criteria

> **Mini-Lesson:** A leak’s size isn’t measured by its duration alone but by its **drag**—how much it slows your overall cycle and fragments attention.

5.3 Quantifying Leak Impact: The Leak Drag Ratio

To prioritize fixes, calculate your **Leak Drag Ratio (LDR):**

LDR=Minutes Lost to LeaksTotal Minutes Tracked×100\text{LDR} = \frac{\text{Minutes Lost to Leaks}}{\text{Total Minutes Tracked}} \times 100LDR=Total Minutes TrackedMinutes Lost to Leaks×100

- **Minutes Lost to Leaks:** Sum of all logged leak activities in a day.
- **Total Minutes Tracked:** From your Day 1 audit (Chapter 4) or ongoing tracker.

An LDR of **10%** means one in ten minutes vanish in leaks. Your goal: drive LDR below **5%** within two weeks.

5.4 Exercise: Identifying Your Top 3 Leaks

1. **Review Your Day 1 Audit:** Scan for categories or context notes marked ▯/●.

2. **List All Leak Activities:** E.g., "Instagram scroll: 15 min," "Meeting drift: 20 min."
3. **Aggregate by Type:** Tally total minutes per leak type.
4. **Rank:** Identify the three leaks with highest total drag.
5. **Document:** In your journal, create a "Top 3 Leak" table:

Leak	Type	Total Minutes	% of Day	First-Order Cause
Instagram Scrolling	Distraction	45	3.1%	Unchecked notifications
Email Checking	Email Triage	60	4.2%	Inbox open all day
Meeting Overrun	Meeting Drift	50	3.5%	No strict agenda/timer

5.5 Root Cause Analysis: The "5 Whys" Method

For each top leak, probe deeper:

1. **State the Leak:** e.g., "I lost 45 min to Instagram."
2. **Why?** "Because I get notifications and check impulsively."
3. **Why?** "Because my phone is within arm's reach."
4. **Why?** "Because I leave it on my desk while working."
5. **Why?** "Because I haven't established a designated charging station."

After five levels, you reach an actionable root cause: "Phone placement and notification rules lead to distraction leaks." Record each "5 Whys" chain in your journal.

5.6 Designing Micro-Interventions

With causes exposed, craft targeted fixes—small experiments that block or shorten leaks. Aim for interventions you can implement **today**:

Leak	Root Cause	Micro-Intervention
Instagram Scrolling	Notifications + phone proximity	Silent mode + phone in drawer during deep-work blocks
Email Checking	Inbox always open	Use “Email Windows”: two 15-min blocks at 10 AM/4 PM
Meeting Overrun	No strict timer or agenda	Add a “5 min wrap-up” agenda item; enforce auto-end

> **Exercise:** For each top leak, list at least **two** micro-interventions. Choose one to trial immediately.

5.7 Case Study: Alex and the Email Abyss

Background: Alex, a product manager, found email triage consumed nearly **2 hours** daily. She felt tethered to her inbox, losing momentum on strategic work.

5 Whys Analysis:

1. **Why** check email constantly? – “Fear of missing urgent messages.”
2. **Why** fear missing messages? – “Team doesn’t use Slack reliably.”
3. **Why** no Slack adoption? – “No clear channel guidelines.”
4. **Why** lack guidelines? – “No onboarding for communication protocols.”
5. **Why** no onboarding? – “Company growth outpaced process design.”

Micro-Interventions:

- **Email Windows:** Block 9–9:30 AM & 3–3:30 PM for email.
- **Auto-Responder:** “For urgent matters, ping me on Slack; otherwise, I reply during windows.”
- **Slack Revival:** Draft and share simple channel usage guide with team.

Results (Week 2):

- Email time dropped from 120 min to **45 min** (LDR ↓ from 8% to 3%).
- Deep Work recovered by an extra 1 hour/day.
- Team clarity improved—fewer “urgent” emails.

5.8 Tool Spotlight: Leak-Sealing Automations

Automation isn’t just for routine tasks; you can also use it to enforce micro-interventions:

- **Notification Quarantine:**
  - **Zapier Automation:** At the start of a deep-work block, trigger “Do Not Disturb” on Mac/Windows & mute phone via smart-home integration.
- **Email Scheduling:**
  - **Gmail Schedule Send:** Buffer outgoing emails; send only at designated windows.
- **Meeting Timer Bot:**
  - **Clockwise + Google Meet Add-On:** Automatically trim meetings to 25 min or 50 min, adding 5-min breaks.

> **Metric: Automation Leak Coverage (ALC)** – the percentage of top 3 leaks managed by an automation.

ALC=Leaks with at least one automation fixTop 3 Leaks×100\text{ALC} = \frac{\text{Leaks with at least one automation fix}}{\text{Top 3 Leaks}} \times 100ALC=Top 3 LeaksLeaks with at least one automation fix×100

Aim for **≥66%** ALC by Day 7.

5.9 AI Prompt: Leak Reduction Coach

Engage your AI assistant to brainstorm and refine interventions. Try:

pgsql
CopyEdit
```
"I lose 45 minutes daily to Instagram notifications and impulsive
checks. My root cause is phone proximity and unchecked alerts. Propose
five creative strategies—technological, behavioral, or environmental—
to cut this leak by at least 70%. Include one strategy that uses AI."
```

Record the AI's top three suggestions, choose one, and schedule its implementation.

5.10 Ritual: The Leak-Detection Scan

Adopt a daily 2-minute ritual at day's end to catch emerging leaks:

1. **Open Journal (10s):** Flip to today's page.
2. **Scan Categories (30s):** Note any unexpected drain in each bucket.
3. **Highlight New Leaks (30s):** Mark any >5 min surprises.
4. **Quick Fix Decision (30s):** Commit to one micro-intervention for tomorrow.
5. **Close with Gratitude (20s):** Thank yourself for the insight.

Over a week, this ritual surfaces nascent leaks before they become entrenched.

5.11 Common Pitfalls & Proactive Fixes

Pitfall	Fix
Over-engineering interventions	Start with one simple fix per leak, refine later
Intervention Fatigue	Rotate fixes to maintain freshness; celebrate small wins

Ignoring Secondary Leaks	After top 3 are down, scan for the next-highest drag sources
Underestimating Emotional Anchors	Pair interventions with positive rewards (break, treat)
Failing to Measure	Always log minutes saved and re-calculate LDR daily

---

5.12 Reflection & Preparation for Chapter 6

You've now:

- Identified and classified your top time leaks
- Calculated your Leak Drag Ratio (LDR)
- Performed root-cause analysis with the "5 Whys"
- Designed and trialed micro-interventions
- Leveraged automations and AI to seal leaks
- Established a daily leak-detection ritual

Next journey: In **Chapter 6: Peak-State Mapping**, you'll chart the ebb and flow of your mental energy across the day—so you can sequence high leverage tasks into your optimal performance windows.

Tonight's Journal Questions:

1. *"Which micro-intervention created the biggest gain today?"*
2. *"What new leak emerged that I hadn't noticed before?"*
3. *"How will I test a countermeasure for that leak tomorrow morning?"*

By answering these, you ensure each leak you patch further fortifies the dam of your time wealth.

Chapter 6: Peak-State Mapping

> "Your mind has natural peaks and valleys. Align your deepest work with the peaks, and let the valleys be your launchpads for recovery."
> —Dr. Justin Goldston

6.1 Understanding Peak States

Every individual's cognitive energy ebbs and flows in predictable rhythms. These rhythms—shaped by circadian biology, personal habits, and environmental factors—define your **peak states** (when you're at your sharpest) and **trough states** (when energy sags). By mapping these states, you can schedule high-leverage activities during peaks and reserve low-stakes or restorative tasks for troughs. This alignment multiplies your Deep Work effectiveness and guards against burnout.

- **Peak State Traits:** Heightened focus, creative insight, efficient decision-making.
- **Trough State Traits:** Mental fog, ease of distraction, lower resistance to breaks.

6.2 The Science Behind Cognitive Rhythms

Neuroscience reveals two key drivers of your daily energy cycle:

1. **Circadian Alertness Curve**
   - Governed by the suprachiasmatic nucleus responding to light cues.
   - Typical pattern: Low in early morning, peaks mid-morning, dips after lunch, smaller peak late afternoon, declines into evening.
2. **Ultradian Performance Cycles**
   - 90–120 minute spikes of focus followed by 20–30 minute dips.
   - Known as the Basic Rest–Activity Cycle (BRAC).

Mini-Lesson: Treat ultradian dips not as failures but as built-in "rest breaks." Planning mini-rituals around these dips leverages natural physiology for sustained performance.

6.3 Mapping Your Unique Energy Profile

Step 1: Select Your Tracking Period

- **Duration:** 7 consecutive days to capture weekday and weekend variance.
- **Granularity:** Log energy level every hour on a 1–5 scale (1 = exhausted, 5 = peak focus).

Step 2: Logging Protocol

- **Tool Options:**
    - Manual: Paper journal or Notion with hourly prompts.
    - Automated: A simple mobile form (Typeform) linked via Zapier to your dashboard.
- **Prompt:** "Rate my current mental energy from 1–5."

Step 3: Contextual Notes

- Add brief context for each rating: "Post-lunch slump," "After 15-min walk," "Third espresso."

6.4 Visualizing Your Energy Landscape

Once data is collected, create two key visualizations:

1. **Daily Energy Curve** (Line Chart)
    - X-axis: Hours of day (e.g., 6 AM–10 PM)
    - Y-axis: Average energy rating
2. **Weekly Heatmap**

- Rows: Days of week
- Columns: Hourly slots
- Cells: Color-coded energy levels (□ high, □ moderate, □ low)

These visuals reveal consistent peaks—your prime windows for Deep Work—and recurring troughs—ideal for breaks or low-stakes tasks.

6.5 Exercise: Your First Peak-State Map

1. **Log Energy for 7 Days:** Follow sections 6.3 and 6.4.
2. **Draft Visuals:** Use your chosen tool to plot curves and heatmaps.
3. **Identify Top Three Peak Windows:** Note the hours with consistently 4+ ratings.
4. **Highlight Three Trough Windows:** Note hours with consistently ≤2 ratings.

Journal Prompt:
"What surprised me about my peak and trough timings? How do these align (or clash) with my current schedule?"

6.6 Sequencing Tasks to Natural Rhythms

Armed with your Peak-State Map, restructure your day:

Task Type	Peak Hours	Trough Hours
Deep Creative	Highest energy windows	—
Analytical Work	Mid-range peaks	—
Admin & Email	Trough or low-moderate periods	Ideal for repetitive, low-focus tasks

Learning & Research	Moderate peaks	Optional, if mentally restorative
Rest & Recovery	—	Directly follow trough dips

Action Step: In your calendar, drag existing tasks into these new slots. Use colored labels (e.g., red = deep work, blue = admin) to visualize alignment.

6.7 Case Study: Javier's Time Realignment

Background: Javier, a data scientist, forced himself into "5 AM deep work," mimicking popular routines, but felt groggy and unproductive. His Peak-State Map revealed actual peaks at 10 AM–12 PM and 4–6 PM, with a pronounced trough at 2–3 PM.

Intervention:

- **Moved deep-coding sessions** to 10 AM–12 PM.
- **Scheduled team calls** and emails at 2 PM (trough).
- **Reserved 4–6 PM** for data exploration and creative ideation.

Outcome (Week 2):

- Reported a 50% boost in code velocity during deep sessions.
- Felt energized after trough-based breaks instead of fighting fatigue.
- Reduced "forced" 5 AM alarms and increased overall satisfaction.

6.8 Ritual: The Peak-State Primer

To kick off each peak window with maximum clarity:

1. **Hydration Check (10s):** Drink a full glass of water.
2. **Posture Reset (10s):** Stand, stretch arms overhead.

3. **Sensory Cue (10s):** Play a specific 5-second audio tone or song snippet.
4. **Intention Statement (15s):** Quietly state, “I harness this peak to deliver my best.”

Linking this primer to your designated peak windows conditions your mind to recognize and fully engage with high-energy periods.

6.9 Integrating Ultradian Breaks

Within each peak window, embed ultradian-paced micro-breaks:

- **Protocol:** After 90 minutes of focused work, take a 20-minute reset.
- **Activities:** Short walk, breathing meditation, light stretching, or a restorative snack.
- **Tracking:** Log break quality on a scale of 1–3 (1 = unfocused wandering, 3 = deep rest).

Metric: Ultradian Compliance Rate (UCR)

UCR=Number of properly timed breaksRecommended breaks per day×100\text{UCR} = \frac{\text{Number of properly timed breaks}}{\text{Recommended breaks per day}} \times 100UCR=Recommended breaks per dayNumber of properly timed breaks×100

Aim for **100%** compliance in Week 1, then optimize break activities based on quality ratings.

6.10 AI Prompt: Personalized Peak-State Coach

Use your AI assistant to refine your schedule. Try:

css
CopyEdit

```
“I have peak windows at 10–12 PM and 4–6 PM, and trough at 2–3 PM.
Suggest a daily schedule that aligns my top-priority tasks with these
windows, incorporates ultradian breaks, and includes my recurring
meetings. Provide a color-coded 8-hour block plan.”
```

Paste the AI’s suggestion into your calendar and adjust as needed for real-world constraints.

6.11 Common Pitfalls & Solutions

Pitfall	Solution
Forcing Productivity in Natural Troughs	Resist the urge—use troughs for genuine rest or low-stakes tasks.
Ignoring Weekend Variances	Map weekends separately; don't force weekday routines onto different rhythms.
Overlooking External Constraints	Balance ideal windows with fixed obligations; carve mini-peaks within constraints.
Skipping Ultradian Breaks	Automate break reminders via calendar events or AI nudges.
Static Mapping	Update your Peak-State Map every 30 days to account for seasonal, lifestyle changes.

6.12 Reflection & Setting Up Chapter 7

You have now:

- Uncovered your unique daily and weekly energy rhythms.
- Learned to schedule tasks in harmony with natural peaks and troughs.
- Embedded ultradian breaks to maintain sustained performance.
- Employed AI to craft an optimized, personalized calendar.
- Established primers and rituals to enter peak states swiftly.

Next destination: In **Chapter 7: Block Scheduling Essentials**, you'll master thematic batching—grouping similar tasks into cohesive, inviolable time blocks—further reinforcing your alignment with peak states and Infinite Cycles.

Tonight's Journal Prompts:

1. *“Which peak window transformation yielded the biggest surprise today?”*
2. *“How did my ultradian breaks affect my focus and mood?”*
3. *“What adjustment will I make to my 10 AM–12 PM block tomorrow?”*

By answering these, you cap off your mapping experiment and prime yourself for deliberate, block-based design.

Chapter 7: Block Scheduling Essentials

> “Time blocks are like gravity wells for focus—they pull your attention in and hold it there until the work is done.”
> —Dr. Justin Goldston

7.1 The Power of Thematic Batching

Block scheduling, or “time batching,” groups similar tasks into contiguous time blocks. This minimizes context-switching overhead—those hidden fractions of attention lost every time you pivot from one activity to another. By dedicating each block to a single theme (e.g., writing, meetings, learning), you tap into the brain’s natural affinity for sustained focus.

- **Cognitive Benefit:** Reduces the “restart penalty” after each switch, boosting effective focus time by up to 30%.
- **Emotional Benefit:** Creates psychological safety—a clear container in which your work lives, reducing decision fatigue.
- **Practical Benefit:** Simplifies calendar design, making commitments visible at a glance.

7.2 Identifying Your Core Block Types

Not every block needs identical length or frequency. Common block categories include:

Block Type	Purpose	Typical Duration

Deep Work	High-cognitive tasks (writing, coding, analysis)	60–120 minutes
Shallow Work	Quick, administrative tasks (email, billing, updates)	15–30 minutes
Creative Play	Ideation, sketching, free-association exercises	45–60 minutes
Collaboration	Meetings, calls, brainstorming sessions	30–90 minutes
Learning & Growth	Reading, courses, skill practice	30–60 minutes
Recovery & Ritual	Breaks, meditation, walking	10–30 minutes
Social & Networking	Mentoring, coffee chats, lunches	30–60 minutes

> **Mini-Lesson:** Aim for no more than **4 block types per day** to keep your schedule manageable.

7.3 Crafting Your Weekly Block Template

A weekly template provides consistency while preserving flexibility. To build yours:

1. **Define Priorities:** List your top 3–5 weekly goals (e.g., finish Chapter 8 draft, launch email campaign).
2. **Allocate Deep Work Blocks:** Place 3–4 deep-work blocks on days when your Peak-State Map (Chapter 6) indicates high energy.
3. **Schedule Shallow Work Daily:** Reserve 15–30 minute windows for email and admin—ideally at trough times.
4. **Insert Creative Play & Learning:** Bookend deep sessions with creative or learning blocks to prime or reinforce new neural pathways.
5. **Embed Recovery Blocks:** After every 90–120 minutes of focus, schedule a 15–20 minute recovery.

6. **Plan Collaboration Windows:** Group meetings together—e.g., Tuesdays and Thursdays 1–3 PM—preventing them from fragmenting your week.

Exercise: Create a 5-day template in your calendar tool. Use color-coding:

- **Red = Deep Work**
- **Blue = Shallow Work**
- **Green = Creative & Learning**
- **Gray = Recovery**
- **Yellow = Collaboration**

7.4 Tools & Tips for Effective Block Scheduling

- **Digital Calendars:** Google Calendar, Outlook, and Apple Calendar all support color-coded events and recurring blocks.
- **Time-Blocking Apps:**
  - **SkedPal:** Dynamically shifts blocks based on your priorities and emerging tasks.
  - **Clockwise:** Auto-moves flexible blocks to create larger focus windows.
- **Visual Overlays:** Use Notion or Trello boards with "Week at a Glance" templates to map blocks visually outside your calendar.
- **Block Buffer:** Always reserve a 5–10 minute buffer at the end of each block to wrap up and prepare for the next.

Tip: Label blocks with clear verbs: e.g., "Write Intro Section," not just "Writing."

7.5 Exercise: Pilot Your First Week of Blocks

1. **Implement Your Template:** Activate the 5-day template in your calendar.

2. **Run a "Dry-Run" Day:** Treat one day as a simulation—follow blocks loosely and note friction points.

3. **Adjust Durations:** If you frequently overrun or underrun, tweak block lengths by 5–15 minutes.

4. **Log Adherence:** In your journal, mark each block as:

    - ✅ Completed on time

    - ☐ Overran by X minutes

    - 🚫 Interrupted

5. **Reflect:** After the day, compute your **Block Completion Rate (BCR):**
 BCR=Number of Blocks Completed as ScheduledTotal Blocks×100\text{BCR} = \frac{\text{Number of Blocks Completed as Scheduled}}{\text{Total Blocks}} \times 100BCR=Total BlocksNumber of Blocks Completed as Scheduled×100
 Aim for **≥80%** in your first trial.

7.6 Case Study: Naomi's Content Creation Blocks

Background: Naomi, a blogger and podcaster, struggled to find focus amid sporadic recording sessions and ad-hoc writing spurts.

Block Schedule Implementation:

- **Deep Work (Writing):** Mondays/Wednesdays 9–11 AM
- **Creative Play (Podcast Ideation):** Tuesdays 2–3 PM
- **Collaboration (Interview Calls):** Thursdays 1–3 PM
- **Shallow Work (Outreach & Emails):** Daily 8:30–9 AM
- **Recovery (Walk & Journal):** 11–11:20 AM after deep work

Results (Week 1):

- **BCR:** 85% (interrupted only by urgent interview reschedules)
- **Output Increase:** Completed two blog drafts vs. one previously.
- **Stress Reduction:** Reported feeling "less reactive" and "in control."

7.7 Measuring and Optimizing Block Adherence

Your BCR is a leading indicator of how well blocks fit real life. To continually optimize:

1. **Weekly Review (Day 7):** Chart BCR each day; identify blocks with BCR < 70%.
2. **Root Cause Analysis:** For low-adherence blocks, ask:
   - Were start/end times realistic?
   - Did interruptions stem from unclear boundaries?
   - Was the block's theme too broad?
3. **Refine Blocks:**
   - Shorten excessively long blocks.
   - Split mixed-purpose blocks into two distinct ones.
   - Add "Do Not Disturb" rules to protect critical slots.

Metric Spotlight: Average Block Overrun (ABO)

ABO=∑Minutes OverrunTotal Blocks\text{ABO} = \frac{\sum \text{Minutes Overrun}}{\text{Total Blocks}} ABO=Total Blocks∑Minutes Overrun

Aim for **<10 minutes** average overrun.

7.8 AI Prompt: Block Schedule Optimizer

Let your AI assistant sharpen your template. Try:

pgsql
CopyEdit
```
"I have recurring tasks: writing, email, meetings, and ideation. My
Peak-State Map shows peaks at 10–12 and 4–6 PM. Propose a weekly block
schedule that: 1) maximizes deep work in peak windows, 2) batches
meetings on Tuesdays/Thursdays, 3) includes two creative play blocks,
and 4) allocates daily recovery. Present the schedule as a table with
times and color codes."
```

Integrate the AI's suggestions, then test and adjust based on real-world constraints.

7.9 Ritual: Block Launch & Closure

To signal the start and end of each block:

1. **Launch Ritual (30s):**
   - Silence notifications (5s)
   - Quick stretch (10s)
   - State block intention aloud (15s)
2. **Closure Ritual (30s):**
   - Log outcome in journal (10s)
   - Rate focus quality 1–5 (10s)
   - Take a 5-second mental "reset" breath (10s)

These micro-rituals bookend your blocks, enhancing psychological ownership and providing clear transition points.

7.10 Common Pitfalls & Proactive Fixes

Pitfall	Fix

Overcrowding Your Schedule	Leave 10–20% of each day unblocked for ad-hoc tasks
Rigid Blocks, No Flexibility	Build “floating” blocks for spillover tasks or unexpected wins
Vague Block Definitions	Use specific outcomes (e.g., “Draft 500 words”) vs. generic “Write”
Ignoring Energy Data	Always align new templates with your latest Peak-State Map
Skipping Rituals	Automate reminders to run launch/closure rituals

---

7.11 Integrating Blocks with Infinite Cycles & Peak States

Block scheduling isn’t standalone—it amplifies the Infinite Cycle (Chapter 2) and Peak-State alignment (Chapter 6):

- **Cycle Integration:** Each thematic block becomes a self-contained Infinite Cycle: intention → action → feedback → renewal.
- **State Alignment:** Deep-work blocks lock into your peak windows; recovery blocks coincide with known troughs.

> **Insight:** When blocks, cycles, and peaks converge, you create a “sweet spot” of maximum productivity and well-being.

7.12 Reflection & Preview of Chapter 8

You’ve now:

- Defined and implemented core block types
- Built and piloted your weekly block template
- Measured BCR and ABO for continuous refinement

- Leveraged AI to optimize your schedule
- Embedded rituals to mark block transitions
- Ensured alignment with cycles and energy peaks

Next up: In **Chapter 8: Micro-Rituals for Seamless Transitions**, you'll design and deploy a suite of ultra-brief rituals—cues, gestures, and prompts—that glide you effortlessly between blocks and mental states, preserving focus and preventing drift.

Tonight's Journal Prompts:

1. *"Which block felt most natural, and which felt forced?"*
2. *"Where did I experience the largest overrun, and why?"*
3. *"What micro-ritual can I test to improve my next Deep Work launch?"*

By answering these, you conclude your block-scheduling experiment and set the stage for fluid transitions ahead.

Chapter 8: Micro-Rituals for Seamless Transitions

> "The richness of your workday lies not only in the blocks you schedule but in the gateways you build between them."
> —Dr. Justin Goldston

8.1 Why Transitions Matter

Even the most meticulously scheduled day can unravel at the seams if you neglect the moments between tasks. Each transition—ending one block and beginning the next—is a hidden decision point. Without clear cues and mental resets, you accrue **transition debt**, manifesting as lost seconds that snowball into wasted minutes and fractured focus. Micro-rituals are the antidote: bite-sized ceremonies (5–45 seconds) that punctuate your day, signaling to your brain that one mode of being has ended and another begins.

- **Cognitive Benefit:** Sharp boundaries reduce cognitive residue from prior tasks.

- **Emotional Benefit:** Rituals confer psychological closure and renewal, alleviating guilt or task hangover.
- **Physiological Benefit:** Brief movement or breathing resets stress hormones and primes neurochemistry for the next block.

8.2 The Anatomy of a Micro-Ritual

A robust micro-ritual typically includes four elements:

1. **Signal Cue (5–10s):** A perceptual trigger—sound, touch, or visual change—that marks the transition point.
2. **Release Action (10–15s):** A brief act that "lets go" of the preceding block—physical stretch, jotting a completion note.
3. **Intention Setting (10–15s):** A concise affirmation of purpose for the upcoming block—spoken, whispered, or mentally visualized.
4. **Calibration Breath (5–10s):** A slow inhalation/exhalation cycle that synchronizes mind and body.

> **Mini-Lesson:** Even a 20-second ritual, if executed consistently, rewires your nervous system to anticipate and embrace mental shifts.

8.3 Designing Your Micro-Ritual Library

To cover every transition type, build a set of **three to five** distinct rituals:

Transition Type	Example Ritual Elements	Duration
Deep Work → Recovery	1) Play a 3-note chime; 2) Stand & shake out arms; 3) Whisper "Rest now, recharge"; 4) 2 deep breaths.	30s
Recovery → Deep Work	1) Tap desk twice; 2) Roll shoulders; 3) State "Focus now"; 4) 2 grounding breaths.	25s

Block A → Block B	1) Snap fingers; 2) Close eyes & exhale fully; 3) Visualize new task; 4) Inhale for 5s.	20s
Email → Call	1) Mute notifications; 2) Lean forward in chair; 3) Affirm "Speak with clarity."	15s
Meeting End → Next Deep Work	1) Press "End Call" button; 2) Stretch neck & back; 3) Whisper "Return to flow"; 4) 3s breath.	35s

Exercise: Draft at least three micro-rituals of your own, naming each (e.g., "The Anchor Drop," "The Focus Bell," "The Reset Stretch").

8.4 Signal Cues: Harnessing Environmental Triggers

Signal cues can be external (devices, sounds) or internal (gestures, mantras).

- **Audio Triggers:** A specific 1-second chime, a short song clip, or a voice note played via your AI assistant.
- **Tactile Triggers:** Pressing a specific key combination (e.g., Caps Lock twice), snapping fingers, or touching a textured object.
- **Visual Triggers:** Changing your wallpaper or shifting a physical token on your desk (a stone, figurine, or card).
- **Temporal Triggers:** Aligning transitions with clock-based anchors, such as "at every quarter hour."

> **Tip:** Consistency is key—use the same cue each time for a given transition so the association strengthens quickly.

8.5 Release Actions: Letting Go of the Past Block

A release action creates psychological and physiological distance from the completed task:

- **Movement:** A brief stretch targeting tension areas (shoulders, neck, wrists).

- **Journaling:** A single-sentence log: "Completed: [Block Name] – Key outcome: _____."
- **Gesture:** Clenching and releasing your fist, or flicking a wrist upward.
- **Sound:** Exhaling through pursed lips to produce a soft "haaa" release sound.

Exercise: Practice three release actions now—note which feels most "complete" before moving on.

8.6 Intention Setting: Inviting the Next Task

Clarifying your aim primes your prefrontal cortex for goal-directed behavior:

- **Affirmation Template:** "In this [Block Type], I will [Concrete Outcome]."
  - E.g., "In this Deep Work block, I will draft the introduction's first 300 words."
- **Visualization:** Picture the successful end-state—your completed task, the satisfaction you'll feel.
- **Mantra:** A brief phrase capturing the block's essence (e.g., "Write with courage," "Solve with clarity," "Connect with empathy").

AI Prompt:

css
CopyEdit

```
"Generate three crisp intention statements for a 60-minute code review session, each under 10 words, that inspire focus and thoroughness."
```

8.7 Calibration Breaths: Resetting Your Neurochemistry

Breathwork is the quickest route to shifting autonomic states:

- **Box Breath (20s):** Inhale 4s—Hold 4s—Exhale 4s—Hold 4s.
- **4-7-8 Breath (30s):** Inhale 4s—Hold 7s—Exhale 8s.

- **Alternate Nostril (30s):** Close right nostril, inhale left; switch and exhale right; repeat.

Metric: Rapid Reset Efficiency (RRE)

RRE=Self-reported post-ritual focusPre-ritual distraction level×100\text{RRE} = \frac{\text{Self-reported post-ritual focus}}{\text{Pre-ritual distraction level}} \times 100 RRE=Pre-ritual distraction levelSelf-reported post-ritual focus×100

Track RRE over your first 5 uses of a new ritual; aim for an average **≥150%**, indicating a strong reset effect.

8.8 Exercise: Implementing a Full Micro-Ritual

1. **Choose a Common Transition:** e.g., Deep Work → Shallow Work.
2. **Apply Your Ritual:** Execute signal cue → release action → intention → calibration breath.
3. **Log Outcomes:** Rate on a 1–5 scale:
   - Ease of transition
   - Speed of mental shift
   - Loss of focus avoided
4. **Refine:** Adjust elements (longer release, different cue) and repeat tomorrow.

Journal Prompt:
"Which component of my ritual felt most transformative, and which felt clunky or unnecessary?"

8.9 Case Study: Lina's Meeting-to-Deep-Work Ritual

Background: Lina, a project lead, found herself mentally lingering on meeting discussions, hampering her afternoon writing blocks.

Ritual Design:

- **Cue:** A 2-second "ding" via Teams at meeting end.
- **Release:** Stand, roll shoulders, and stretch arms wide (15s).
- **Intention:** Whisper, "Write with clarity and focus" (10s).
- **Breath:** Three cycles of Box Breath (20s).

Results (Week 1):

- Reported a **70% reduction** in "sticky thoughts" from meetings.
- Afternoon writing output increased by 40%.
- Meeting fatigue feelings dropped from 4/5 to 2/5.

8.10 Ritual Variants for Different Contexts

Context	Ritual Variant
Email → Email	Cue: Open email draft; Release: Shake hands; Intention: "Reply with brevity"; Breath: 4-4-4 Box Breath
Commute → Home	Cue: Park car; Release: Lock car; Intention: "Switch to home mind"; Breath: 4 deep belly breaths
Home → Work (Mornings)	Cue: Put on headphones; Release: Wash face; Intention: "Enter work zone"; Breath: Alternate Nostril
Afternoon Slump → Work	Cue: Stand; Release: 10 squat pulses; Intention: "Push through"; Breath: 4-7-8 method
Learning → Application	Cue: Close book; Release: Tap desk; Intention: "Use what I learned"; Breath: 3 rapid inhales/exhales

Tip: Customize rituals to your environment and role—office, home, laboratory, studio.

8.11 Common Pitfalls & Troubleshooting

Pitfall	Fix
Skipping Rituals Under Pressure	Automate cues—calendar pop-ups or wearable haptic reminders
Rituals Becoming Mechanical	Rotate elements weekly to maintain novelty
Overly Long Rituals Disrupt Flow	Trim rituals to 15–20 seconds maximum
Unclear Intention Statements	Use SMART format (Specific, Measurable, Achievable, Relevant, Time-bound)
Neglecting Physical Release	Prioritize a movement element to reset stress hormones

8.12 Integrating Rituals into Your Time-Wealth System

Micro-rituals intersect with every framework you've built:

- **Infinite Cycles (Chapter 2):** Rituals serve as the **Renewal** phase, ensuring each cycle closes and primes the next.
- **Peak States (Chapter 6):** Ritual primers activate peak-state cues; release rituals signal the start of recovery troughs.
- **Block Scheduling (Chapter 7):** Rituals enforce block boundaries, raising your BCR and lowering ABO.

> **Insight:** Rituals are the glue that bonds your theory to practice—without them, schedule and mindset remain siloed.

8.13 Reflection & Preview of Chapter 9

You've now:

- Crafted a library of micro-rituals tailored to your day
- Anchored rituals in signal cues, release actions, intentions, and breaths
- Measured ritual efficacy via RRE
- Refined rituals through journaling and AI prompts
- Integrated rituals with cycles, peaks, and blocks

Next up: In **Chapter 9: Energy Management & Recovery**, you'll dive deeper into Pomodoro science, mini-break protocols, and advanced recovery strategies—ensuring your system honors both flow and restoration in dynamic equilibrium.

Tonight's Journal Prompts:

1. *"Which ritual created the smoothest transition today, and why?"*
2. *"What transition still feels rough, and how might I tweak its ritual?"*
3. *"Which cue or release action deserves rotating out for freshness?"*

By answering these, you fine-tune your ritual arsenal and prepare for the restoration practices ahead.

Chapter 9: Energy Management & Recovery

> "True productivity isn't about endless push; it's about riding the wave of your focus, then surfing the swell of renewal."
> —Dr. Justin Goldston

9.1 The Dual Imperative: Focus and Restoration

Most productivity systems fixate on output—how much you can do in a block of time. But without deliberate recovery, deep work becomes shallow, and bursts of effort lead to crashes. **Energy management** balances two imperatives:

1. **Maximize Focus:** Sustain high-attention work during peak states.
2. **Optimize Recovery:** Activate restoration processes in troughs to recharge mind and body.

When these forces align, you create a **self-sustaining cycle**: focused work enhances appreciation for breaks, and quality restoration amplifies subsequent focus.

9.2 The Science of Ultradian Rhythms and Pomodoro Variants

Your brain operates in 90–120 minute cycles (ultradian rhythms) punctuated by 20–30 minute dips. Traditional Pomodoro (25/5) approximates these cycles, but you can fine-tune parameters:

Variant	Work Interval	Break Interval	Best For
Classic	25 min	5 min	Beginners, shallow work
Extended	50 min	10 min	Deep analytical tasks
Ultradian	90 min	20–30 min	Maximum flow, complex problem-solving
Microburst	15 min	3 min	Low-energy days, quick sprints
Custom Hybrid	Variable	Proportional	Tailored to individual Peak-State Map rhythms

> **Mini-Lesson:** Aligning your work/break intervals with your personal ultradian data (Chapter 6) yields the highest sustained focus.

9.3 Designing Your Personalized Pomodoro Protocol

Step 1: Reference Your Peak-State Map

- Identify periods of high, moderate, and low energy.

Step 2: Choose an Ultradian-Friendly Variant

- For strong peaks: try 90/20.
- For moderate peaks: try 50/10.
- For low-energy days: start with 15/3 microbursts.

Step 3: Implement and Track

- Use a dedicated timer app (Focus To-Do, Be Focused, or an AI-driven Pomodoro bot).
- Log each cycle's start/end, and note subjective focus quality (1–5 scale) and break satisfaction (1–5 scale).

Step 4: Compute Your Focus-to-Break Ratio (FBR)

FBR=∑Work Minutes∑Break Minutes\text{FBR} = \frac{\sum \text{Work Minutes}}{\sum \text{Break Minutes}}FBR=∑Break Minutes∑Work Minutes

Aim for an FBR that feels energizing—typically between **3:1** and **4:1** for most people.

9.4 Exercise: Trialing Three Variants

1. **Select Three Protocols:** Classic (25/5), Extended (50/10), and one based on your Peak-State Map (e.g., 90/20).
2. **Schedule a Single Work Day:** Divide an 8-hour workday equally among these variants.
3. **Log Rigorously:** For each cycle, record:
    - Focus Quality (1–5)
    - Break Satisfaction (1–5)
    - Energy Upon Return (1–5)
4. **Analyze Results:** Compute average scores and FBR for each variant.

5. **Choose Your Champion:** Select the variant with the best combined Focus + Recovery score for Week 2.

Journal Prompt:
"Which Pomodoro variant felt most natural, and which yielded the highest energy rebound? Why?"

9.5 Advanced Recovery Strategies

Beyond timed breaks, deep recovery involves **physical**, **mental**, and **environmental** techniques:

9.5.1 Physical Restoration

- **Movement Breaks:** Short sequences of yoga stretches, desk push-ups, or walking ladders stimulate blood flow and clear metabolic waste in the brain.
- **Micro-Workouts:** 3–5 minutes of bodyweight exercises—squats, lunges, or calf raises—during longer breaks.
- **Hydration & Nutrition:**
  - **Hydration Ritual:** Drink 250 ml of water at each break's start.
  - **Snack Strategy:** Protein-rich or low-glycemic snacks (nuts, Greek yogurt) to stabilize energy.
- **Posture Reset:** Use posture-correcting tools (lumbar cushions, standing desks) and perform one chest-opening stretch per break.

9.5.2 Mental Restoration

- **Mindfulness Micro-Sessions:** 2–5 minutes of guided meditation or focused attention on breathing to reduce cognitive residue.
- **Creative Diversions:** Brief doodling, listening to ambient music, or quick free-writing prompts unrelated to work.
- **Gratitude Pauses:** Jot down one thing you're grateful for to shift perspective and release stress.

9.5.3 Environmental Restoration

- **Nature Window:** Spend at least one break per hour gazing at or walking near greenery.
- **Sensory Reset:** Use background soundscapes (birdsong, white noise) or aromatherapy with essential oils (peppermint for alertness, lavender for calm).
- **Workspace Modulation:** Adjust lighting—warm hues for recovery breaks, cool bright light for deep work.

Metric: Recovery Quality Score (RQS)

RQS=Average Break Satisfaction×Average Energy Upon Return5\text{RQS} = \frac{\text{Average Break Satisfaction} \times \text{Average Energy Upon Return}}{5} RQS=5Average Break Satisfaction×Average Energy Upon Return

Track RQS daily; target **≥16** on a 25-point scale (5 + 5 for both metrics across most breaks).

9.6 Exercise: Building Your Recovery Menu

1. **List Five Techniques** from each category (Physical, Mental, Environmental).
2. **Select Three Favorites**—one per category—to rotate through breaks.
3. **Design a Break Routine:** For a 10-minute break, combine:
   - **2 minutes** hydration + hydration ritual
   - **3 minutes** movement micro-workout
   - **3 minutes** mindfulness or creative diversion
   - **2 minutes** gratitude or sensory reset
4. **Pilot for Two Days:** Log RQS after each break and adjust components to maximize scores.

Journal Prompt:
"Which recovery elements felt most restorative, and which need refinement or replacement?"

9.7 Case Study: Priya's Hybrid Recovery Protocol

Background: Priya, a financial analyst, felt drained by mid-afternoon despite following a 50/10 Pomodoro. Her RQS averaged a low **8/25**, and Energy Upon Return hovered around **2/5**.

Intervention: She built a hybrid break routine:

- **Physical (2 min):** Standing desk calf raises + neck rolls.
- **Mental (3 min):** 2-minute breathing meditation (4-7-8) + 1 minute free-writing.
- **Environmental (3 min):** Walk to a nearby plant-filled atrium and listen to recorded birdsong.
- **Gratitude (2 min):** Three gratitude entries in her mobile journal.

Outcome (Week 1):

- **RQS** jumped from 8 to **17**.
- **Energy Upon Return** averaged **4/5**.
- Afternoon Deep Work output increased by **60%**.

9.8 AI Prompt: Personalized Recovery Guide

Let AI curate a bespoke recovery routine. Try:

pgsql
CopyEdit
```
"I work in data analysis with long 90/20 cycles. Suggest a 10-minute
recovery routine combining physical, mental, and environmental
techniques that can be done in a standard office setting without
special equipment."
```

Select the top three AI-suggested elements and integrate them into your next break.

9.9 Ritual: The Break Protocol

Codify your break routine into a **five-step ritual** to automate its execution:

1. **Alert Cue (5s):** A distinct chime or phone vibration.
2. **Hydration & Snack (2 min):** Drink water and have a prepared snack.
3. **Movement Micro-Work (3 min):** Perform pre-chosen exercise sequence.
4. **Mindful Reset (3 min):** Guided breathing or creative pause.
5. **Gratitude & Transition (2 min):** Log gratitude and preview next block's intention.

Over time, this structured ritual becomes as automatic as your work cycles, ensuring you never skip restoration.

9.10 Common Pitfalls & Proactive Fixes

Pitfall	Fix
Skipping Breaks When Busy	Automate lockout—calendar "busy" slots and focus-mode settings
Overlong Recovery Leading to Distracted Drift	Set strict end alarms; micro-ritual to close break
Monotonous Routine Causes Apathy	Rotate recovery menu weekly; introduce novelty
Inadequate Environment for Recovery	Pre-arrange recovery "kit" (earbuds, snack station, plant)
Neglecting Hydration & Nutrition	Batch-prep snacks and keep a full water bottle at hand

---

9.11 Integrating Recovery with Your System

Energy Management & Recovery ties into your broader Time-Wealth system:

- **Infinite Cycles (Ch. 2):** Recovery is the **Feedback** phase that informs your next Intention.
- **Peak States (Ch. 6):** Schedule more immersive recovery during known trough windows.
- **Blocks (Ch. 7):** Embed Recovery Blocks immediately after extended focus blocks.
- **Micro-rituals (Ch. 8):** Use the Break Protocol as your micro-ritual for transitions.

Insight: When recovery is as intentional as work, you sustain high performance without burnout—true time-wealth in action.

9.12 Reflection & Preview of Chapter 10

You have now:

- Experimented with Pomodoro and ultradian-tuned protocols
- Designed and tracked your personalized recovery routines
- Measured FBR and RQS to optimize focus and rejuvenation
- Integrated AI and case-study insights to refine your approach
- Codified a Break Protocol ritual to automate restoration

Next exploration: In **Chapter 10: Digital Boundaries & Detox**, you'll establish guardrails against distraction—setting "no-phone" zones, crafting auto-replies, and automating silences—so you can protect the space you've created for focused work and deep rest.

Tonight's Journal Prompts:

1. *"Which recovery strategy provided the greatest lift, and how can I replicate it consistently?"*
2. *"Where did my energy still dip unexpectedly, and what additional tactic can I apply?"*
3. *"How will I tweak my next FBR target based on today's outcomes?"*

By answering these, you solidify your energy-management framework and gear up for digital boundary mastery ahead.

Chapter 10: Digital Boundaries & Detox

> "Your attention is the soil in which your best work grows. Protect it from toxic inputs so your time-wealth garden can flourish."
> —Dr. Justin Goldston

10.1 Why Digital Boundaries Are Non-Negotiable

In an era of endless pings, badges, and scrolls, your devices can become Trojan horses for distraction. Without deliberate **digital boundaries**, every notification is an intrusion on your finite attention budget. Establishing guardrails not only preserves focus during Deep Work but also safeguards restorative space during Recovery Blocks. Intentional "detox" windows recalibrate your relationship with technology, preventing creeping time poverty and digital burnout.

- **Cognitive Cost:** Each notification can steal up to 23 minutes of regained focus after interruption.
- **Emotional Cost:** Constant connectivity fuels stress, anxiety, and FOMO (Fear of Missing Out).
- **Health Cost:** Blue-light exposure and endless scrolling erode sleep quality and mental well-being.

10.2 Mapping Your Digital Distraction Landscape

Before silencing the noise, catalog your biggest offenders:

Distraction Vector	Mechanism	Typical Daily Drag
Social Media	Infinite feed, autoplay videos	60–120 minutes

Email & Chat Apps	Badge counts, real-time threads	45–90 minutes
News & Aggregators	Breaking alerts, algorithmic push	30–60 minutes
System Notifications	OS updates, reminders, pop-ups	15–30 minutes
Unmanaged Tabs	Tab overload, multitasking	20–40 minutes
Background Apps	Auto-play videos, audio autoplay	5–15 minutes

> **Exercise:** Over one full day (outside your 24-hour audit), note every notification that distracts you. Tally total minutes lost and list them under the Distraction Vector column.

10.3 Designing Your No-Phone Zones

A **No-Phone Zone** is a physical or temporal space where your phone is off-limits. These zones reinforce presence in key contexts:

1. **Spatial Zones:**
    - **Bedroom:** Phone stays on a charging dock across the room.
    - **Desk Perimeter:** Phone in a drawer or on airplane mode during work.
    - **Dining Table:** No devices allowed during meals or social time.
2. **Temporal Zones:**
    - **Deep Work Blocks:** Phone in Do Not Disturb (DND) with only essential calls allowed.
    - **Recovery Blocks:** Phone in another room to prevent accidental checks.
    - **Morning Ritual (6–7 AM):** Phone stays untouched until after your first ritual.
    - **Evening Wind-Down (8–9 PM):** All notifications silenced; no screens.

Exercise: Define three spatial and three temporal No-Phone Zones for your schedule. Document them in your journal and commit to strict adherence for the next three days.

10.4 Crafting Auto-Replies & Status Messages

When you silence incoming messages, let colleagues and connections know you're "in the zone." Auto-replies maintain courtesy while enforcing boundaries:

Email Auto-Reply Template:

pgsql
CopyEdit

```
Subject: [Out of Inbox]
Hello,
I'm currently focused on deep work and will check email twice today at
10:00 AM and 4:00 PM.
If your matter is urgent, please mark it "CRITICAL" in the subject
line or ping me on Slack.
Thank you for your patience!
—Justin
```

-
- **Chat Status Message (Slack/Teams):**

  🚀 **In Deep Work** | Back at 4:00 PM | Please DM "URGENT" for emergencies

- **SMS Auto-Reply (iOS/Android):**

  "I'm currently in a focused session. I'll respond at [time]. If it's urgent, please call me."

Exercise: Configure at least two auto-replies (email and one chat app) and test them. Log any inbound messages to see if urgent flags are used appropriately.

10.5 Automating Silences with Technology

Modern devices offer built-in and third-party tools to enforce digital detox:

Tool	Functionality	Configuration Tip
iOS Focus Modes	Custom DND profiles, auto-replies, home screen filters	Create a "Work" Focus activating during Deep Work
Android Digital Wellbeing	App timers, wind-down schedules, grayscale mode	Set social apps to 15-minute daily timers
Freedom/Cold Turkey	Cross-device app/website blocking	Schedule recurring block sessions
RescueTime FocusTime	Auto-blocks distracting sites during focus periods	Sync with calendar events
Slack Do Not Disturb	Scheduled silences per channel	Mute non-essential channels for Deep Work

> **Exercise:** Pick two tools—one built-in, one third-party—and configure them to block your top two Distraction Vectors during Deep Work and Recovery Blocks.

10.6 Exercise: Full Digital Detox Day

1. **Plan Your Detox:** Select one 6-hour window (including a Deep Work block and a Recovery block).
2. **Enforce Boundaries:**
    - Activate No-Phone Zones.
    - Enable Focus/DND modes.
    - Turn on site/app blockers.
3. **Execute & Log:** At the end of the window, record:
    - Total notifications suppressed

    - Minutes saved (notifications avoided × average regain time)
    - Subjective focus level (1–5)
    - Mood improvement score (1–5)

4. **Journal Reflection:**
    - "How did it feel to be free from pings?"
    - "Which boundary was hardest to uphold?"
    - "What surprised me about my productivity or mindset?"

10.7 Case Study: Zoe's Notification Overhaul

Background: Zoe, a UX designer, was derailed by constant banner alerts—averaging 90 interruptions per day. Her focus score hovered at 2/5.

Interventions:

- **Spatial Boundary:** Placed phone in office safe during work hours.
- **Temporal Boundary:** Set Slack DND from 9–11 AM & 3–4 PM.
- **Auto-Replies:** Configured email and Teams with clear deep-work statuses.
- **App Blocking:** Used Cold Turkey to block social media sites.

Results (Week 1):

- Interruptions ↓ 95% (from 90 to ~5 per day).
- Focus Score ↑ 4/5.
- **Project Output:** Completed a UI prototype a full day ahead of deadline.

10.8 AI Prompt: Boundary-Enforcement Architect

Use AI to generate boundary rules and messages:

sql
CopyEdit

```
"I get pulled into Slack threads and Instagram 50 times per day.
Propose a set of 5 configurable Focus Modes (names, schedules, allowed
apps) and draft auto-reply messages for each mode, ensuring clarity
and politeness."
```

Review AI's proposals, select the top three, and implement them as named Focus Modes on your device.

10.9 Ritual: The Digital Transition Sweep

At the end of each Deep Work block or Recovery block, perform a **40-second sweep** to reinforce boundaries:

1. **Visual Check (10s):** Confirm phone is in its No-Phone Zone.
2. **Focus Mode Toggle (10s):** Manually switch your device to the correct Focus profile.
3. **App Audit (10s):** Close all non-essential browser tabs and apps.
4. **Mind Cue (10s):** Whisper, "Boundaries secure, mind calm."

This ritual creates a hard reset—every 60–90 minutes—so you never drift back into distraction.

10.10 Common Pitfalls & Solutions

Pitfall	Fix
Accidental Breaks in Focus Modes	Use "Lock" features or require passcode to exit Focus Mode

Rigid Boundaries Clash With Team Needs	Communicate schedules clearly; negotiate shared "urgent" channels
Forgetting to Re-Enable Boundaries	Automate via calendar rules or use IFTTT/Zapier to toggle modes
Boundary Fatigue	Schedule occasional "open" windows; treat as reward for discipline
Multi-Device Inconsistency	Sync Focus Modes across phone, tablet, laptop via cloud profiles

---

10.11 Integrating Digital Boundaries with Your Time-Wealth System

Digital boundaries amplify every component of your system:

- **Infinite Cycles (Ch. 2):** Boundaries protect your **Focused Action** and ensure **Immediate Feedback** isn't derailed by pings.
- **Peak States (Ch. 6):** Silence amplifies peak-state performance; curated breaks reinforce trough recovery.
- **Block Scheduling (Ch. 7):** Blocks become inviolable sanctuaries, not digital free-for-alls.
- **Micro-Rituals (Ch. 8):** The Digital Transition Sweep ritual closes and opens each block with authority.
- **Energy & Recovery (Ch. 9):** Detox periods double as restorative intervals, boosting RQS and FBR.

Insight: Boundaries are the architecture that holds your entire time-wealth edifice aloft; without them, even the best routines collapse under the weight of distraction.

10.12 Reflection & Preview of Chapter 11

You've now:

- Cataloged your biggest digital distractions and their daily drag
- Established spatial and temporal No-Phone Zones
- Crafted and tested auto-replies and status messages
- Automated silences with built-in and third-party tools
- Executed a full digital detox window and logged its impact
- Integrated boundaries with rituals, cycles, peaks, and blocks

Next exploration: In **Chapter 11: Designing Your 30-Day Journal**, you'll fuse all these elements—metrics, prompts, reflections—into a lean, powerful daily template that tracks progress, surfaces insights, and sustains momentum throughout your entire month-long journey.

Tonight's Journal Prompts:

1. *"Which boundary felt most liberating, and which required the greatest effort?"*
2. *"How many interruptions did I prevent, and what did I do with the reclaimed time?"*
3. *"What one digital habit will I refine tomorrow to deepen my focus?"*

By answering these, you seal today's gains and prime your journal for tomorrow's breakthroughs.

Chapter 11: Designing Your 30-Day Journal

> "A journal is the compass that guides your voyage through time—capturing your data, your discoveries, and your dedication."
> —Dr. Justin Goldston

11.1 Why a Structured Journal Is Your North Star

A well-crafted journal does far more than record events; it **crystallizes insights**, **anchors commitments**, and **traces progress** across days, weeks, and months. When you track metrics, reflections, and action plans in a consistent format, you build a reliable mirror: one that reflects both your successes and your blind spots. Over 30 days, this mirror reveals patterns too subtle for memory alone, empowering you to iteratively refine your time-wealth system.

- **Accountability:** Writing down intentions increases the likelihood of follow-through by over 80%.
- **Self-Awareness:** Daily entries spotlight emerging habits, emotional reactions, and shifting priorities.
- **Momentum:** A visible record of wins—no matter how small—fuels motivation and combats inertia.
- **Data Richness:** Structured logs accumulate into actionable datasets for AI analysis and long-term planning.

11.2 Core Components of Your Daily Journal Template

To balance brevity with depth, each day's page should include six key sections:

Section	Purpose	Length Estimate
Date & Day Count	Contextual anchor (e.g., Day 12 of 30)	1 line
Time-Wealth Metrics	TWS, LEM, LDR, FBR, RQS, TUR	1–2 lines with values
Block & Ritual Adherence	BCR, ABO, Ritual RRE	1 line summary
Top Insight & Surprises	What stood out today?	2–3 sentences
Key Wins & Gratitude	Three micro-wins and three gratitude entries	Bullet list (6 items)
Next-Day Commitments	Three SMART intentions & micro-interventions	Bullet list (3 items)

Mini-Lesson: Limiting sections prevents overwhelm and ensures consistency—vital for sustaining a 30-day habit.

11.3 Building Your Journal Template in Tools of Choice

Option A: Analog Notebook

- **Layout:** Pre-print or hand-draw a two-page spread per day.
- **Advantages:** Tactile engagement, deeper cognitive encoding.
- **Considerations:** Manual aggregation and digitization for charts.

Option B: Digital Document

- **Platforms:** Notion, Evernote, OneNote, or Google Docs.
- **Template Setup:** Create a recurring page template with fields for each section.
- **Advantages:** Easy duplication, searchability, attachment of charts/screenshots.
- **Considerations:** Screen friction—use keyboard shortcuts or voice-to-text for speed.

Option C: Spreadsheet

- **Columns:** Date, TWS, LEM, LDR, FBR, RQS, TUR, BCR, ABO, RRE, Insights, Wins, Gratitude, Commitments.
- **Advantages:** Immediate data aggregation and charting.
- **Considerations:** Less narrative space for reflections.

Exercise: Choose your medium and build the empty template before Day 1. Time yourself—setup should take no more than 30 minutes.

11.4 Setting Up Automation & Reminders

To ensure you never miss a journal entry:

1. **Calendar Alerts:** Schedule a daily recurring event titled "Journal Check-In" at a consistent time (e.g., 6 PM).

AI Prompts: Use an AI assistant to send you journal prompts:

markdown
CopyEdit
```
"At 6 PM daily, remind me:
1. Enter today's metrics.
2. Describe the top insight.
3. List three wins and gratitudes.
4. Commit to three SMART intentions for tomorrow."
```

2.
3. **Zapier Integration (Digital Template):**
   - Trigger: Calendar event ends →
   - Action: Duplicate your Notion/Google Doc template and email you the link.
4. **Physical Tickler:** For notebooks, keep your journal on your desk or bedside table as a visual cue.

Metric: Journal Completion Rate (JCR)

JCR=Days with Full Entries30×100\text{JCR} = \frac{\text{Days with Full Entries}}{30} \times 100 JCR=30Days with Full Entries×100

Aim for **≥90%** by Day 30.

11.5 Exercise: Pilot Your Day 1 Entry

1. **Gather Today's Data:** Pull metrics from your dashboard (TWS, LEM, etc.).
2. **Fill Each Section:**
   - Date & Day Count

    - Insert all metrics
    - Note BCR, ABO, Ritual RRE
    - Reflect: "I was surprised that…"
    - List: Wins & Gratitude
    - Commit: "Tomorrow, I will…"

3. **Timebox:** Complete the entry within **10 minutes**.
4. **Reflect on the Process:** "Which section took longest? Which felt most insightful?"

Journal Prompt:
"How did this structured reflection differ from informal notes? What adjustments will speed up Day 2?"

11.6 Weekly & Midpoint Check-Ins

Beyond daily logs, embed two deeper review rituals:

Week 1 Review (Day 7):

- **Aggregate Metrics:** Calculate weekly averages of TWS, LDR, RQS, JCR.
- **Trend Analysis:** Plot simple line charts for each metric.
- **Reflection:** Write a 200-word summary:
    - What improved?
    - What stagnated?
    - Which interventions had the biggest impact?

Midpoint Meta-Analysis (Day 15):

- **Heatmap Your Metrics:** Visualize daily variations across 15 days.

- **Pivot or Persevere:** Decide which experiments to double down on and which to retire.
- **Re-set Goals:** Craft three revised or new SMART goals for Days 16–30.

AI Prompt (Midpoint):

CopyEdit

“I have 15 days of journal data: [paste aggregated metrics]. Provide a concise mid-point report with three high-impact recommendations for the next 15 days.”

yaml
CopyEdit

```
---

### 11.7 Case Study: Marcus's Journal-Driven Transformation
**Background:** Marcus, a startup founder, struggled with weekend
productivity slumps and inconsistent rituals. His initial JCR was only
**50%** by Day 7, and his TWS hovered at 20%.

**Interventions:**
- Switched from loose journaling to a tight Notion template.
- Automated prompts via Slackbot at 6 PM daily.
- Added a weekly 30-minute group review with an accountability
partner.

**Results (Day 15):**
- **JCR** rose to **95%**.
- **TWS** climbed to **35%**.
- He reclaimed weekend mornings for creative sprints, boosting morale
and momentum.

---

### 11.8 Leveraging AI for Deep Reflections
Use AI to mine richer insights from your journal:

- **Prompt for Hidden Patterns:**
```

“Analyze my last 7 journal entries and identify three recurring bottlenecks and two emerging strengths. Suggest interventions for each bottleneck.”

markdown
CopyEdit

```
- **Prompt for Inspiration:**
```

“Based on today’s top insight and wins, craft a short motivational paragraph to fuel my journal entry tomorrow.”

yaml
CopyEdit

```
Store AI outputs in a “Journal Insights” section or a separate doc for later review.

---

### 11.9 Tool Spotlight: Data Visualization for Journals
Integrate your daily logs into dashboards:

- **Notion + Charts Plugin:** Embed bar charts for weekly comparisons.
- **Google Sheets + Data Studio:** Connect daily rows to visualize time-wealth curves, leak drag trends, and recovery quality.
- **Airtable Interfaces:** Build a custom “Journal Dashboard” view with graphs, calendar heatmaps, and record galleries.

> **Exercise:** Link your Day 1–7 entries to a simple chart. Observe one early trend and journal about its implications.

---

### 11.10 Ritual: The Journal Seal
Make journaling its own micro-ritual to signal mental closure for the day:

1. **Desk Clean Sweep (30s):** Tidy workspace, align tools, clear any loose paper.
```

2. **Journal Invocation (10s):** Open to today's page and read yesterday's commitments.
3. **Entry Execution (5–10 min):** Complete the template.
4. **Signature & Seal (10s):** Sign your name and tap the page corner—an "official" close.
5. **Mindful Exhale (5s):** Close eyes, exhale fully, and whisper "Day sealed, tomorrow awaits."

This ceremony transforms journaling from a chore into an honored practice.

11.11 Common Pitfalls & Remedies

Pitfall	Remedy
Template Overkill	If entries exceed 15 minutes, remove or simplify one section
Journal Fatigue	Alternate between digital and analog modes weekly
Data Entry Errors	Use dropdowns or predefined metric formulas to reduce typing
Neglecting Reflection Depth	Schedule a bi-weekly "deep dive" session for extended writing
Skipping Midpoint Review	Automate calendar invite and dedicated focus time for Day 15

11.12 Integrating the Journal with Your Time-Wealth Ecosystem
Your journal is the **central nervous system** of the entire 30-day journey:

- **Infinite Cycles (Ch. 2):** Record each cycle's LEM and renewal insights.

- **Toolkit (Ch. 3):** Log tool performance and automation coverage.
- **Audits & Leaks (Chs. 4–5):** Document evolving leak profiles and LDR improvements.
- **Peaks & Blocks (Chs. 6–7):** Chronicle block adherence, ABO, and Peak-State data.
- **Rituals & Recovery (Chs. 8–9):** Capture RRE, RQS, and recovery notes.
- **Boundaries (Ch. 10):** Track boundary adherence and interruption counts.

> **Insight:** A robust journal ties all modular practices into a single, coherent narrative—revealing the story of your time-wealth evolution.

11.13 Reflection & Preview of Chapter 12
You have now:
- Defined and constructed a daily journal template
- Automated prompts, reminders, and template creation
- Completed your first entry and fine-tuned the process
- Embedded weekly and midpoint reviews with AI assistance
- Turned journaling into a celebrated micro-ritual
- Integrated your journal into every aspect of your system

Next up: In **Chapter 12: Week 1 – Awareness & Reflection**, you'll launch the first phase of your 30-day journal journey—executing the baseline audit exercises, mapping insights, and celebrating your inaugural week's micro-wins.

> **Tonight's Journal Prompts:**
> 1. *"How did today's journal entry reveal one unexpected pattern?"*
> 2. *"Which metric surprised me most, and why?"*
> 3. *"What adjustment will I make to tomorrow's template for greater clarity?"*

By answering these, you lock in Day 1's learnings and prepare to dive deeply into Week 1's awareness phase.

End of Chapter 11

Chapter 12: Week 1 – Awareness & Reflection

> "Awareness is the lantern that illuminates hidden patterns; reflection is the mirror that reveals their deeper meaning."
> —Dr. Justin Goldston

12.1 The Purpose of Week 1

Week 1 lays the bedrock of your time-wealth journey. In these seven days, you will:

1. **Execute the Baseline Audit** (Chapter 4) over 24 hours.
2. **Identify & Quantify Time Leaks** (Chapter 5) across multiple days.
3. **Map Peak States** (Chapter 6) to anchor your blocks.
4. **Pilot Block Scheduling** (Chapter 7) and **Micro-Rituals** (Chapter 8).
5. **Test Recovery Protocols** (Chapter 9) and **Digital Boundaries** (Chapter 10).
6. **Begin Journaling** (Chapter 11) each evening.

By systematically layering these practices, you'll transform raw data into actionable insights—and celebrate the first micro-victories that fuel momentum.

12.2 Day 1: Deep Audit & Initial Insights

Morning:

- **Pre-Audit Ritual:** Centering breath, manifesto recital, tool check.

- **Launch Audit:** Auto-track digital activity and manually log offline moments in 15 min intervals.

Afternoon:

- **Midpoint Scan:** At 2 PM, run a quick Leak-Detection Scan (Chapter 5.9) to flag emerging drags.
- **Peak Check:** Record energy rating (Chapter 6) at lunchtime; note any unexpected troughs or peaks.

Evening:

- **Audit Analysis:** Compute Total Minutes per bucket, TUR, and preliminary LEM.
- **Journal Entry:**
    - Day 1 of 30
    - Metrics: TUR, initial TWS (if you completed a focused block), early LEM.
    - Insight: “I was most surprised by how much time I spent on…”
    - Wins: “Completed 24-hour audit,” “Noted peak at…” “Closed phone drawer.”
    - Commitments: “Tomorrow, I will…” (e.g., implement first micro-intervention for top leak).

12.3 Day 2: Leak Sealing & Peak Alignment

Morning:

- **Implement Top Leak Fixes:** For your three highest-drag leaks, activate your chosen micro-intervention and automation.
- **Micro-Rituals:** Use your Deep Work → Recovery ritual after the first block.

During Day:

- **Block Pilot:** Follow your weekly template's Day 2 schedule (Chapter 7), aligning Deep Work with known peaks.
- **Recovery & Breaks:** Apply your 10-min Break Protocol (Chapter 9).

Evening:

- **Leak Drag Recalculation:** Compute Day 2's LDR; compare to Day 1.
- **Peak-State Reflection:** Note any shifts in your energy curve; did interventions improve peak clarity?
- **Journal Entry:**
    - Metrics: Day 2 LDR, FBR (first Pomodoro variant), RQS.
    - Insight: "Sealing my Instagram leak freed up…"
    - Wins & Gratitude: Three micro-wins, three gratitudes.
    - Commitments: "Tomorrow, I'll adjust my 90/20 cycle to 75/15 because…"

12.4 Day 3: Block Refinement & Ritual Stress-Test

Morning:

- **Block Adherence Check:** Compute Day 2's BCR and ABO; tweak block durations or buffer lengths based on overrun data.
- **Ritual Audit:** Rate your micro-rituals' RRE; refine cues or release actions that felt weak.

Daytime:

- **Flexible Block Insertion:** If an urgent task appears, slot it into a "floating" block rather than breaking an existing one.
- **Digital Boundary Reinforcement:** Run a midday Digital Transition Sweep to reaffirm Focus Mode.

Evening:

- **Mid-Week Metric Snapshot:**
  - Average TWS (Days 1–3)
  - Average LEM, LDR, FBR, RQS
  - Current JCR (Days 1–3)
- **Journal Entry:**
  - Insight: "My BCR improved by X%, but ABO rose due to…"
  - Wins & Gratitude: Emphasize resilience ("I honored my Digital Detox zone")
  - Commitments: "I will schedule a "meeting-free" afternoon block tomorrow."

12.5 Day 4: AI-Enhanced Reflection & Adaptation

Morning:

AI Prompt Session:

pgsql
CopyEdit

```
"Analyze my Days 1–3 journal entries. Identify two recurring
bottlenecks and propose micro-interventions. Highlight any emerging
strengths to amplify."
```

-
- **Implement:** Select one AI-driven suggestion and integrate it into today's schedule.

Daytime:

- **Peak-State Reconfirmation:** Re-log energy ratings at each peak/tough pivot. Adjust Deep Work start times if necessary.
- **Pomodoro Tweaks:** Switch to the variant that performed best in your Day 2 trial.

Evening:

- **Journal Entry:**
    - Metrics: updated FBR, new micro-intervention impact (minutes saved).
    - Insight: “AI suggested I batch all emails into one block, which…”
    - Wins & Gratitude
    - Commitments: “I will test an alternative break activity (creative diversion) tomorrow.”

12.6 Day 5: Peer Accountability & Collaborative Review

Morning:

- **Accountability Partner Check-In:** Share your Week 1 progress metrics and insights in a 15-minute call or message.

Daytime:

- **Collaborative Block:** If you have a mentor or partner, schedule a joint Deep Work session using your micro-ritual for transition.

Evening:

- **Mid-Point Team Debrief:**
    - Present Week 1’s key metrics.
    - Solicit feedback on interventions.
- **Journal Entry:**
    - Insight: “My partner recommended…”
    - Wins & Gratitude

- Commitments: “Based on feedback, tomorrow I’ll…”

12.7 Day 6: Metacognitive Check & Emotional Overlay

Morning:

- **Emotion Mapping:** At three points today, rate emotional state (Energized/Neutral/Drained) and tag your log with color codes □/□/●.

Daytime:

- **Cycle Efficiency Focus:** Intentionally slow one Infinite Cycle to test deeper feedback: lengthen Renewal pause to 30 seconds with added reflection.

Evening:

- **Journal Entry:**
    - Metrics: LEM (with extended Renewal), average emotional map.
    - Insight: “I noticed that after my extended Renewal, my next cycle was…”
    - Wins & Gratitude
    - Commitments: “I will apply the extended Renewal in tomorrow’s final audit.”

12.8 Day 7: Weekly Synthesis & Celebration

Morning:

- **Weekly Review Ritual (Chapter 11.6):** Aggregate all metrics into a chart—TWS, LDR, LEM, FBR, RQS, BCR, ABO, RRE, JCR.

Daytime:

- **Mindful Retreat:** Allocate a two-hour block for deep reflection—no digital tools, only pen, paper, and your weekly dashboard print-out.

Evening:

- **Journal Entry (Extended):**
  - **Weekly Averages & Trends:**
    - TWS: ___ → target for Week 2.
    - LDR: ___ → micro-intervention ROI.
    - Peak vs. Trough consistency.
  - **Key Lessons (5 bullets):** What this week taught you about your habits, energy, and tools.
  - **Top Three Wins:** Celebrate the biggest breakthroughs (metric or qualitative).
  - **Gratitude Audit:** List three people or events you're grateful for this week.
  - **Week 2 Preview:** Identify three experiments or refinements for the next phase (e.g., "test 90/20 cycle," "automate two more leaks," "expand No-Phone Zone to evening").
  - **Commitment to Celebration:** Plan a small reward—coffee treat, walk in nature, or call with a friend.

12.9 Case Study: Week 1 Transformation of Alice

Baseline (Day 1):

- TWS: 18%
- LDR: 12%
- BCR: 60%

- RQS: 10/25
- JCR: 1/7

Interventions Executed:

1. Moved phone to drawer during deep work.
2. Piloted 50/10 Pomodoro.
3. Created three micro-rituals and refined two.
4. Automated email batching.
5. Journaled nightly with AI prompts.

End of Week 1:

- TWS: 30% (+12%)
- LDR: 5% (−7%)
- BCR: 85% (+25%)
- RQS: 18/25 (+8)
- JCR: 7/7 (100%)

Alice's Reflection:

> "I went from feeling scattered to intentional. The biggest shift for me was sealing my email leak—it unlocked two extra hours of deep work that felt sacred. Celebrating small wins kept me motivated, and seeing every metric improve made the effort tangible. Week 1 proved that time-wealth isn't a myth—it's a series of conscious choices."

12.10 Common Pitfalls & Proactive Solutions

Pitfall	Fix

Overwhelm from Multiple Experiments	Limit to two high-impact experiments per day; schedule others later
Data Fatigue	Automate metric aggregation; focus journal on top three insights
Inconsistent Rituals	Tie rituals to calendar events; automate reminders
Skipping Midweek Reflection	Block 15 min on Day 4 for a mini-review
Neglecting Emotional Well-Being	Include emotional tags in every journal entry; address red zones

---

12.11 Integrating Week 1 into the Bigger Picture

Week 1's work lays the scaffolding for deeper optimization in Weeks 2–4:

- **Week 2 (Intentional Design):** You'll redesign your blocks, deepen AANT alignment, and refine micro-rituals.
- **Week 3 (AI-Augmented Optimization):** You'll scale automations, predictive scheduling, and habit-loop analytics.
- **Week 4 (Sustainable Habits & Resilience):** You'll cement triggers-actions-rewards, social accountability, and seasonal planning.
- **Days 29–30 (Consolidation):** You'll integrate all data into a master dashboard and craft your infinite RRULE roadmap.

> **Insight:** A strong Week 1 awareness phase ensures that every subsequent experiment is grounded in real data, personal rhythm, and tested practices—minimizing guesswork and maximizing growth.

12.12 Reflection & Preview of Chapter 13

You have now:

- Completed the 7-day baseline audit and reflections.
- Sealed major leaks and celebrated metric improvements.
- Piloted blocks, rituals, Pomodoro variants, and digital boundaries.
- Journaled nightly, leveraged AI insights, and engaged accountability partners.
- Synthesized your first-week data into clear wins and Week 2 commitments.

Next destination: In **Chapter 13: Week 2 – Intentional Design**, you'll harness these insights to refine your daily structure—crafting deeper, more AANT-aligned blocks, transition rituals, and recovery protocols optimized for your personal rhythm.

Tonight's Journal Prompts:

1. *"What three patterns from Week 1 will shape my Week 2 experiments?"*
2. *"Which intervention had the highest ROI, and how can I amplify it?"*
3. *"What one metric will be my Non-Negotiable North Star for Week 2?"*

By answering these, you anchor your Week 2 design in the luminous clarity of Week 1's hard-won awareness.

Chapter 13: Week 2 – Intentional Design

> "Awareness shows you where you are; intentional design charts the course to where you want to be."
> —Dr. Justin Goldston

13.1 The Goal of Week 2

While Week 1 was about shining the lantern on your current habits, Week 2 transforms those insights into **purposeful structures**. You'll redesign and reinforce your system—crafting blocks that align tightly with your peak states, deepening AANT-informed rituals, and refining recovery and boundary strategies for maximal impact. By week's end, you'll have a cohesive, personalized blueprint that turns your calendar into a launchpad for high-leverage work and restorative balance.

13.2 Day 8: Block & Ritual Overhaul

Morning:

- **Block Template Revision (Ch. 7):** Using Week 1's BCR and ABO data, adjust durations and placements of Deep Work, Shallow Work, and Recovery blocks. Incorporate one new "Floating Block" for unplanned high-priority tasks.
- **Ritual Library Expansion (Ch. 8):** Select two new micro-rituals to test—for example, a "Focus Bell" chime or a short body scan meditation.

Midday:

- **AANT Timing Experiment:** Schedule one Deep Work block using the AANT-derived "learning window" (peak + 10% buffer). Apply your most effective launch ritual to enter flow quickly.

Afternoon:

- **Recovery Protocol Refinement:** Based on Week 1 RQS data, swap one recovery activity (e.g., replace meditation with guided imagery) and log the RQS change.

Evening:

- **Journal Entry:**
    - Metrics: Day 8 BCR, ABO, RRE for new rituals, updated RQS.
    - Insight: "Extending my Deep Work to 75 min aligned with my energy peak at…"
    - Wins & Gratitude: Bullet three successes.
    - Commitments: "Tomorrow, I will test a different AANT timing variant and two new leak fixes."

13.3 Day 9: Micro-Optimization of AANT Cycles

Morning:

- **Cycle Adjustment:** For each Infinite Cycle (Ch. 2), add one AANT-enhanced element—an AI-generated mnemonic cue or a practice sentence that reinforces neuroplasticity ("My brain adapts and thrives with each moment of focus").

During Day:

- **Pomodoro Variant Selection:** Adopt the hybrid variant suggested by your Day 2 trial—if 50/10 performed best, schedule two consecutive 50/10 sessions followed by one 90/20 cycle.
- **Digital Boundary Audit:** Introduce a brief "App Triage" block at midday: 10 minutes dedicated to reviewing and closing browser tabs.

Evening:

- **Journal Entry:**
    - Metrics: FBR with new Pomodoro variant, minutes spent in App Triage block, Day 9 LEM.
    - Insight: "The mnemonic cue boosted my focus because…"
    - Wins & Gratitude & Commitments: "I will automate one App Triage routine using Zapier tomorrow."

13.4 Day 10: AI-Augmented Habit Loop Engineering

Morning:

- **Habit-Loop Analytics (Ch. 9):** Review habit-tracking data to identify one habit loop (trigger–action–reward) that needs strengthening—e.g., your morning planning ritual.

Midday:

AI Prompt for Habit Refinement:

pgsql
CopyEdit
```
"I perform a morning planning ritual but often skip the reward phase.
```

```
Suggest three creative, AI-generated rewards tied to this habit that reinforce dopamine and pleasure."
```

-
- **Implement:** Choose one reward (e.g., a 2-minute celebratory stretch sequence) and embed it into your morning routine.

Afternoon:

- **Leak Re-Evaluation:** Recompute LDR; note impact of yesterday's Zapier automation on your top leak.

Evening:

- **Journal Entry:**
    - Metrics: Habit completion rate for morning ritual, new LDR, updated RQS.
    - Insight: "The AI-suggested reward made me look forward to breakfast because..."
    - Wins & Gratitude & Commitments: "Tomorrow, I'll introduce a new micro-intervention for my secondary leak."

13.5 Day 11: Collaborative Design & Peer Feedback

Morning:

- **Peer Review Session:** Share your revised block template, micro-ritual designs, and recovery protocols with an accountability partner or small group. Solicit two pieces of actionable feedback.

During Day:

- **Collaborative Deep Work Block:** Schedule a co-working session (virtual "focus cowork" or in-person). Apply your launch ritual at the start and close ritual at the end.

Evening:

- **Journal Entry:**
    - Metrics: Shared session duration, focus quality rating, partner-rated accountability score (1–5).
    - Insight: “Working alongside my partner helped me…”
    - Wins & Gratitude & Commitments: “Tomorrow, I’ll integrate one peer suggestion into my Break Protocol.”

13.6 Day 12: Environmental & Sensory Enhancements

Morning:

- **Workspace Upgrade:** Introduce one environmental tweak—e.g., a small plant, a daylight lamp, or a textured mat for foot grounding.

Daytime:

- **Sensory Reset Testing:** During recovery breaks, cycle through three soundscapes (ambient nature, binaural beats, white noise) and track RQS for each.

Evening:

- **Journal Entry:**
    - Metrics: RQS by soundscape, overall RQS, Day 12 LEM.
    - Insight: “The rainforest sounds increased my break satisfaction by…”
    - Wins & Gratitude & Commitments: “I will standardize my preferred soundscape for all recovery blocks tomorrow.”

13.7 Day 13: Dynamic Scheduling & Predictive Blocks

Morning:

Predictive Scheduling: Use AI to forecast tomorrow's top tasks based on Week 1 & 2 journal data:

perl
CopyEdit
```
"Based on my last 12 days of focus and productivity metrics, generate a 5-block schedule for tomorrow that maximizes high-leverage tasks in my peak windows and balances recovery."
```

-
- **Import:** Accept the AI's schedule into your calendar as a guide, then tweak for known meetings.

During Day:

- **Dynamic Block Testing:** When unplanned tasks arise, evaluate whether to fit them into existing blocks or swap float blocks; log each decision's impact on your LEM.

Evening:

- **Journal Entry:**
    - Metrics: Alignment percentage (AI vs. actual), LEM, Block Swap count.
    - Insight: "Predictive scheduling improved my morning Deep Work by…"
    - Wins & Gratitude & Commitments: "Tomorrow, I will refine my float block criteria."

13.8 Day 14: Mid-Phase Meta-Review & Celebration

Morning:

- **Midpoint Synthesis Ritual:** Spend 20 minutes reviewing Days 8–13 journal entries and metrics. Chart trends for each key indicator (TWS, LDR, BCR, RQS, FBR, LEM).

Midday:

- **Strategic Pause:** Dedicate a 90-minute "mini-retreat" block—no digital devices—focused on envisioning your ideal Week 3 system enhancements.

Afternoon:

- **Plan Week 3:** Based on insights, pre-schedule one new high-impact experiment (e.g., a "digital Sabbath" half-day, introducing social accountability group check-ins, or piloting a new AI habit coach).

Evening:

- **Extended Journal Entry:**
    - **Week 2 Metrics Averages & Shifts:** Compare to Week 1 baselines.
    - **Three Major Learnings:** Summarize in bullet points.
    - **Top Three Wins & Gratitudes:** Celebrate metric improvements and qualitative breakthroughs.
    - **Revised SMART Goals for Week 3:** Craft goals that are specific, measurable, and ambitious (e.g., "Achieve TWS ≥ 40%," "Reduce LDR to ≤ 3%," "Maintain JCR ≥ 95%").
    - **Reward Mapping:** Plan a tangible reward for successful Week 2 execution (e.g., a favorite meal, a nature hike, or a creative hobby session).

13.9 Case Study: Week 2 Evolution of Kamal

Baseline End of Week 1:

- TWS: 24%
- LDR: 7%
- BCR: 80%
- RQS: 15/25

- JCR: 100%

Week 2 Interventions:

1. Redesigned block template with floating blocks.
2. Introduced AI-prompted reward for morning ritual.
3. Tested three new micro-rituals and two new soundscapes.
4. Ran predictive scheduling via AI.
5. Hosted two peer accountability sessions.

Results End of Day 14:

- TWS: 36% (+12%)
- LDR: 4% (−3%)
- BCR: 88% (+8%)
- RQS: 20/25 (+5)
- JCR: 100%

Kamal's Reflection:

> "Week 2 felt like moving from blueprint to construction. The AI schedule was surprisingly accurate, and the new rituals kept transitions feeling fresh. My biggest surge came when I automated rewards—suddenly mornings felt celebratory instead of habitual. Seeing two weeks of data made the improvements undeniable."

13.10 Common Pitfalls & Proactive Fixes

Pitfall	Fix

Experiment Overload	Limit to 1–2 high-impact changes per day; schedule others in Week 3
AI Dependency	Balance AI suggestions with gut instinct; always review before applying
Peer Feedback Paralysis	Implement one peer idea at a time; iterate based on personal data
Environmental Changes Ignored Over Time	Rotate workspace tweaks monthly to maintain novelty
Midweek Burnout	Insert an extra “fun” float block—social call or creative play

---

13.11 Integrating Intentional Design into Your Ecosystem

Week 2’s deliberate redesign cements the systems you began building in Week 1:

- **Infinite Cycles (Ch. 2):** Customized cycles now reflect AANT prompts, AI cues, and enriched rituals.
- **Toolkit (Ch. 3):** Added automations for App Triage and predictive scheduling.
- **Peak & Blocks (Chs. 6–7):** Blocks recalibrated to mirror refined Peak-State Maps and dynamic float slots.
- **Rituals & Recovery (Chs. 8–9):** Ritual library expanded, recovery menu optimized, soundscapes standardized.
- **Boundaries (Ch. 10):** Digital zones and Focus Modes enforced with new automation rules.
- **Journal (Ch. 11):** Template remains constant; entries now reflect deeper Week 2 insights.

> **Insight:** Week 2 is the heart of your transformation—where raw awareness blossoms into resilient, high-performance habits.

13.12 Reflection & Preview of Chapter 14

You have now:

- Overhauled your block and ritual design based on data-driven feedback.
- Intensified AANT-aligned cycles with AI-generated cues and rewards.
- Expanded recovery and environmental strategies for richer breaks.
- Piloted predictive scheduling and collaborative accountability.
- Synthesized two weeks of metrics into clear, ambitious Week 3 goals.

Next frontier: In **Chapter 14: Week 3 – AI-Augmented Optimization**, you'll scale your system by automating deeper habit loops, leveraging predictive analytics for dynamic scheduling, and co-creating customized AI agents that anticipate and guide your time-wealth journey—propelling you beyond manual design into a new era of autonomous productivity.

Tonight's Journal Prompts:

1. *"Which Week 2 experiment had the highest multiplier effect on my metrics?"*
2. *"What one AI agent or automation will I develop for Week 3?"*
3. *"How will I celebrate the completion of Intentional Design?"*

By answering these, you cap your second week with clarity, momentum, and excitement for the intelligent automation that awaits.

Chapter 14: Week 3 – AI-Augmented Optimization

> "When insight meets automation, your system transcends human limits—AI becomes the wind in your sails."
> —Dr. Justin Goldston

14.1 The Mission of Week 3

Week 3 shifts your focus from manual design to **AI-powered amplification**. You'll harness intelligent agents and predictive analytics to:

1. **Automate routine decisions** and reminders.
2. **Dynamically adjust** your schedule based on real-time data.
3. **Reinforce habit loops** with machine-generated cues and rewards.
4. **Scale your system** beyond one-off experiments into an adaptive framework.

By the end of Day 21, you'll have custom AI helpers that anticipate your needs, optimize your blocks on the fly, and surface insights you'd never spot on your own.

14.2 Day 15: Automating Admin & Mundane Tasks

Morning:

- **Identify Admin Chores:** List 3–5 repetitive tasks (e.g., email triage, file organization, status reporting).

AI Prompt & Zapier Script:

diff
CopyEdit
```
"Create a Zap that:
- Every weekday at 9:00 AM,
- Exports yesterday's Toggl report,
- Generates a bullet-point summary via ChatGPT,
- Emails it to me and my accountability partner."
```

-
- **Implement:** Build and test the automation; confirm successful runs.

Afternoon:

- **Admin-Free Block:** Schedule a 60-minute Deep Work block labeled "□ No Admin." AI blocks social apps and email automatically.

Evening:

- **Journal Entry:**
    - Metrics: Admin time saved (minutes) vs. manual baseline.
    - Insight: "The AI summary freed up ____ minutes I spent previously on reporting."
    - Wins & Gratitude
    - Commitment: "Tomorrow, I will automate one more task—perhaps calendar event organization."

14.3 Day 16: Predictive Scheduling in Action

Morning:

- **Data Consolidation:** Export Days 1–15 metrics (TWS, LEM, LDR, BCR) into a single CSV.

AI Prompt for Schedule Generation:

sql
CopyEdit
```
"Using this CSV data, predict my focus quality for each hour of
tomorrow. Propose a 7-block schedule that:
- Maximizes predicted focus quality,
- Respects my fixed obligations,
- Allocates at least two float blocks."
```

-
- **Import & Adjust:** Merge the AI's schedule into your calendar; tweak manually for known events.

Afternoon:

Live Adaptation: When a meeting overruns, trigger an AI recalculation:

pgsql
CopyEdit

```
"Reschedule my remaining blocks to accommodate this 30-min meeting overrun at 3 pm, preserving deep-work alignment with peak states."
```

-

Evening:

- **Journal Entry:**
    - Metrics: Predictive alignment score (percentage of AI-suggested blocks you followed).
    - Insight: "Predictive scheduling aligned ____% of my tasks with my actual energy peaks."
    - Wins & Gratitude & Commitment: "I will refine my input data overnight to improve predictions."

14.4 Day 17: AI-Coached Ultradian & Habit Loops

Morning:

- **Habit Loop Selection:** Choose one emerging habit (e.g., post-block gratitude entry) for coaching.

AI Prompt:

sql
CopyEdit
```
"Coach me through a habit-loop check:
- I performed my gratitude ritual after each Deep Work block,
- Rate my consistency and suggest one micro-adjustment to the trigger or reward."
```

-
- **Implement Adjustment:** If AI recommends adding a visual cue (e.g., a checkmark sticker), apply it immediately.

Daytime:

- **Ultradian Compliance Bot:** Set up an AI-driven timer that adjusts break intervals based on real-time focus ratings:
    - If focus >4/5, extend work by 5 minutes;
    - If focus ≤2/5, shorten work by 5 minutes.

Evening:

- **Journal Entry:**
    - Metrics: New UCR (Ultradian Compliance Rate) and average adjusted cycle length.
    - Insight: "Extending work cycles in high-focus moments gained me ____ additional minutes of Deep Work."
    - Wins & Gratitude & Commitment: "Tomorrow, I'll test an alternative reward phase in this habit loop."

14.5 Day 18: Building a Personalized AI Agent

Morning:

- **Agent Definition:** Decide on a single AI agent role—for example, "Time-Wealth Concierge" that reminds you of rituals, suggests focus windows, and flags leaks.
- **Tool Setup:** Use a no-code AI platform (Make.com, Zapier with OpenAI) to:
    1. Ingest your daily metrics spreadsheet.
    2. At 8 AM, 12 PM, and 4 PM, send tailored Slack or email messages:
        - "Your next peak window is at ____—ready your micro-ritual."
        - "Your current LDR is ____%; consider sealing your email leak now."

Daytime:

- **Interact:** Respond to agent prompts and rate its helpfulness (1–5). Collect feedback for iterative improvement.

Evening:

- **Journal Entry:**
  - Metrics: Agent interaction count and average helpfulness rating.
  - Insight: "My concierge's morning nudge improved my ritual adherence by ____%."
  - Wins & Gratitude & Commitment: "I'll refine its messaging cadence tomorrow to avoid fatigue."

14.6 Day 19: Data-Driven Habit Reinforcement with No-Code ML

Morning:

- **Dataset Preparation:** Compile 19 days of journal metrics into a dataset in Google Sheets.
- **No-Code ML Model:** Use a tool like Google's AutoML Tables to predict which micro-interventions most reliably increase TWS.
- **Interpretation:** Identify the top two interventions (e.g., "laptop lid closure" or "stand-up stretch").

Daytime:

- **Targeted Experiment:** Deploy those two interventions across two successive blocks; compare resulting LEM and RQS to control blocks.

Evening:

- **Journal Entry:**
  - Metrics: Predicted vs. actual impact on TWS and LEM.

- Insight: “The model correctly identified that stretching improved my next cycle’s focus by ____%.”
- Wins & Gratitude & Commitment: “Tomorrow, I’ll introduce a third intervention based on model recommendations.”

14.7 Day 20: Generative AI for Reflection & Planning

Morning:

AI Reflection Prompt:

perl
CopyEdit
```
“Summarize my Week 3 progress in a concise executive briefing of 150 words. Highlight three major wins, two remaining challenges, and one strategic recommendation for next week.”
```

-
- **Review & Refine:** Tweak the AI’s briefing for tone and accuracy; store it as your “Week 3 Snapshot.”

During Day:

Next-Day Planning: Ask AI:

pgsql
CopyEdit
```
“Based on my Week 3 Snapshot and Week 4’s theme of sustainability, propose a 5-block schedule for tomorrow plus one new habit loop to pilot.”
```

-

Evening:

- **Journal Entry:**
  - Metrics: Incorporation rate of AI’s suggestions; compare with your actual schedule adherence.

- Insight: "The Week 3 Snapshot reminded me of ____"
- Wins & Gratitude & Commitment: "I will pilot the new habit loop in tomorrow's first block."

14.8 Day 21: Week 3 Meta-Review & Celebration

Morning:

- **Automated Report Generation:** Trigger your AI agent to compile Days 15–21 metrics into a dashboard: TWS, LDR, UCR, Agent ratings, predictive alignment.

Midday:

- **Community Share-Out:** Post your dashboard snapshot and top insights to your accountability group or social circle for feedback and celebration.

Afternoon:

- **Ritual & Reward:** Block a 90-minute "Innovation Jam"—a creative free-play session—and follow it with your chosen Week 3 reward (e.g., a special meal or nature outing).

Evening:

- **Extended Journal Entry:**
  - **Week 3 Metrics & Trends:** Contrast with Weeks 1 & 2.
  - **Agent Evolution:** Document how your AI concierge and ML models accelerated your growth.
  - **Top Three AI-Driven Breakthroughs:**
    1. Task automation saved ____ hours.
    2. Predictive scheduling boosted TWS by ____%.
    3. Habit-loop reinforcement increased UCR by ____%.

- **New SMART Goals for Week 4:** E.g., "Achieve TWS ≥ 45%, LDR ≤ 2%, automate two more leak types."
- **Celebration Plan:** A tangible milestone event (virtual or in-person) to honor your AI-augmented mastery.

14.9 Case Study: Week 3 Transformation of Sienna

End of Week 2 Baseline:

- TWS: 36%
- LDR: 4%
- BCR: 88%
- RQS: 20/25
- JCR: 100%

Week 3 Interventions & Outcomes:

Intervention	Metric Impact
Admin Automation (Day 15)	Admin time ↓50% (+1.5 hrs Deep Work)
Predictive Scheduling (Day 16)	Alignment ↑80% (TWS ↑3%)
AI Habit Coaching (Day 17)	Habit completion ↑90% (Morning ritual)
Personalized AI Agent (Day 18)	Ritual adherence ↑85%
No-Code ML Insights (Day 19)	UCR ↑15%
Generative AI Reflection (Day 20)	Planning accuracy ↑75%

End of Week 3 Results:

- **TWS:** 42% (+6%)
- **LDR:** 2.5% (−1.5%)
- **BCR:** 92% (+4%)
- **RQS:** 22/25 (+2)
- **JCR:** 100%

Sienna's Reflection:
"Week 3 felt like unlocking a new gear. My AI concierge became less of a novelty and more of a collaborator—nudging me at just the right moments. Automations reclaimed hours I never knew I lost, and predictive schedules guided me into flow before I even felt distracted. It's remarkable how much faster progress can accelerate when your system thinks alongside you."

14.10 Common Pitfalls & Proactive Fixes

Pitfall	Fix
Over-Automating and Losing Agency	Maintain manual overrides; schedule "manual only" blocks weekly
Data Overload from AI Reports	Limit AI briefings to one key insight per metric
Agent Fatigue (Notification Blindness)	Vary messaging cadence; pause agent reminders during high-intensity blocks
Model Drift in Predictive Scheduling	Re-train dataset every 7 days with latest metrics
Neglecting Human Touch in Rituals	Blend AI prompts with personal gestures; avoid fully algorithmic rituals

---

14.11 Integrating AI-Optimization into Your Ecosystem

Week 3's AI enhancements weave into every strand of your time-wealth tapestry:

- **Infinite Cycles:** AI predicts optimal Renewal phases and refines feedback signals.
- **Toolkit:** Automated Zaps, ML models, and bespoke agents become core tools.
- **Peak & Blocks:** Predictive scheduling keeps blocks aligned with real-time energy.
- **Rituals & Recovery:** AI suggests novel cues and restorative variants.
- **Boundaries:** Focus modes toggle automatically based on calendar and behavior.
- **Journal:** AI-generated snapshots and mid-week reports enrich reflections.

> **Insight:** Human intention, when amplified by AI, transforms a rigid system into a living, adaptive organism—continuously learning and improving with minimal manual effort.

14.12 Reflection & Preview of Chapter 15

You have now:

- Automated key workflows and reclaimed hours.
- Employed predictive AI to keep you in flow.
- Co-created habit-loop reinforcements with intelligent agents.
- Built and iterated a personalized AI concierge.
- Leveraged no-code ML to amplify high-impact interventions.
- Used generative AI for executive snapshots and planning.
- Celebrated Week 3's AI-powered breakthroughs.

Next chapter: In **Chapter 15: Week 4 – Sustainable Habits & Resilience**, you'll cement these gains into **enduring systems**—structuring quarterly reviews, embedding social accountability, and designing "digital sabbaths" so that your time-wealth practices persist long after this 30-day sprint.

Tonight's Journal Prompts:

1. *"Which AI augmentation felt most transformative, and why?"*
2. *"What agent or automation will be my 'must-keep' feature going forward?"*
3. *"How will I design a sustainable reward system for ongoing practice?"*

By answering these, you crystallize Week 3's AI magic and prepare to build unshakeable resilience in Week 4.

Chapter 15: Week 4 – Sustainable Habits & Resilience

> "A system only truly serves you when it weathers storms. Resilience is built not in perfect conditions, but through intentional renewal and social scaffolding."
> —Dr. Justin Goldston

15.1 The Objective of Week 4

Having spent three weeks cultivating awareness, designing intentional structures, and supercharging with AI, Week 4 is devoted to **anchoring those gains for the long haul**. You will:

1. Solidify habit loops so they run automatically.
2. Build social and environmental supports to reinforce accountability.
3. Design quarterly and annual review rituals (RRULEs) that prevent backsliding.
4. Integrate "digital sabbaths" and seasonal adjustments for sustainable balance.
5. Map a resilient roadmap that weathers life's unpredictability.

By Day 28 you'll possess a robust, adaptive ecosystem—capable of evolving rather than eroding once the 30-day sprint ends.

15.2 Day 22: Cementing Habit-Loop Mastery

Morning:

- **Habit Audit:** Review all habit loops introduced (rituals, recovery, journaling). Identify three loops where completion < 90%.
- **Loop Reinforcement Exercise:** For each weak loop, strengthen one of the three elements:
    - **Trigger:** Add a physical cue (e.g., place a token on your desk).
    - **Action:** Simplify the behavior (e.g., reduce journaling prompt length).
    - **Reward:** Enhance the payoff (e.g., add a micro-reward like a 30-second dance).

Midday:

- **Social Accountability:** Share your reinforced habit plan with an accountability partner and schedule two check-ins.

Evening:

- **Journal Entry:**
    - Metrics: Updated habit-completion rates, JCR, RRE.
    - Insight: "Strengthening the trigger for my morning ritual boosted completion by…"
    - Wins & Gratitude
    - Commitments: "Tomorrow I will validate two rituals while experimenting with a new physical cue."

15.3 Day 23: Designing the Quarterly Review RRULE

Morning:

- **Introduction to RRULEs:** A recurring rule in iCal VEVENT syntax that schedules repeating events.

Template RRULE:

ruby
CopyEdit
```
BEGIN:VEVENT
RRULE:FREQ=MONTHLY;INTERVAL=3;BYDAY=MO,TU,WE,TH,FR;BYHOUR=10;BYMINUTE=
0;BYSECOND=0
END:VEVENT
```

- This schedules a quarterly review on the next weekday at 10 AM.

Midday:

- **Draft Your Quarterly Agenda:**
    1. Aggregate TWS, LDR, BCR, RQS trends (past quarter).
    2. Evaluate progress on long-term goals.
    3. Reset priorities based on seasonal or life changes.
    4. Plan next quarter's experiments (e.g., new AI tool, boundary tweak).

Evening:

- **Journal Entry:**
    - Insert your custom RRULE for quarterly reviews.
    - Insight: "Planning a quarterly ritual gives me confidence that I won't revert to old habits."
    - Wins & Gratitude & Commitments: "I will test the RRULE by scheduling a mock mini-review next month."

15.4 Day 24: Social Accountability Structures

Morning:

- **Accountability Frameworks:** Choose one or more of:
    - **Peer Pod:** A group of 3–5 fellow time-wealth practitioners for weekly check-ins.
    - **Public Commitment:** Post your key metrics on social media or a blog.
    - **Mentorship Session:** Schedule monthly 1:1 calls with a mentor or coach.

Daytime:

- **Implement Check-In Ritual:**
    - Monday: Share prior week's snapshot in your Peer Pod Slack channel.
    - Wednesday: Accountability partner video call to discuss midweek metrics.
    - Friday: Email your mentor a concise Week 4 summary.

Evening:

- **Journal Entry:**
    - Metrics: Peer Pod engagement (count of interactions), accountability call scores (1–5).
    - Insight: "Public commitment increased my BCR by making me more reluctant to skip blocks."
    - Wins & Gratitude & Commitments: "Tomorrow, I'll invite a new member into my Peer Pod."

15.5 Day 25: Seasonal & Digital Sabbaths

Morning:

- **Concept of Digital Sabbath:** A full or partial day of intentional disconnection—no work tools, minimal digital consumption.

- **Seasonal Planning:** Identify at least one "Sabbath" per month and one per season (e.g., one work-free weekend monthly; a week-long detox each quarter).

Daytime:

- **Plan Your Next Digital Sabbath:**
    - Choose dates (e.g., next Sunday).
    - Define allowed and disallowed activities (e.g., reading physical books ok; no social media).
    - Inform stakeholders via auto-reply:

      "I'm on a Digital Sabbath from [start] to [end], responding on [return date]."

Evening:

- **Journal Entry:**
    - Reflection: "Scheduling my next Sabbath felt like planting a future oasis."
    - Wins & Gratitude & Commitments: "I will honor my first Sabbath by preparing offline activities today."

15.6 Day 26: Embedding Environmental Resilience

Morning:

- **Workspace Resilience Audit:** Ensure your environment supports your system:
    - Backups of digital dashboards.
    - Physical backups: print key habit prompts or keep a "ritual kit" near your desk.
    - Ergonomic check: confirm desk height, chair support.

Daytime:

- **Disruption Drill:** Simulate a common disruption (e.g., unexpected meeting, power outage). Practice your recovery ritual and adaptive block rescheduling:

  "AI, reschedule my blocks around this 45-minute ad-hoc meeting, preserving two deep-work slots."

Evening:

- **Journal Entry:**
  - Metrics: Speed of recovery (minutes to re-enter focus), revised BCR post-disruption.
  - Insight: "My recovery ritual got me back on track in only 5 minutes."
  - Wins & Gratitude & Commitments: "Tomorrow, I'll refine my recovery for multi-hour disruptions."

15.7 Day 27: Integrating Continuous Learning Loops

Morning:

- **Learning Framework:** Dedicate one float block each week to meta-learning about your system—reading related articles, exploring new AI tools, or reviewing academic studies on productivity.
- **Tool Spotlight:** Use RSS feeds or an AI agent that curates one relevant article per week.

Daytime:

- **Apply & Record:** After reading, choose one tactic to pilot immediately (e.g., a new breathing technique, a novel AI prompt).

Evening:

- **Journal Entry:**
  - Metrics: Learning block adherence, implemented tactic's immediate impact on RQS or LEM.
  - Insight: "Applying a new breathing technique improved my Break Protocol RQS by…"
  - Wins & Gratitude & Commitments: "Tomorrow, I'll share this tactic with my Peer Pod."

15.8 Day 28: Week 4 Meta-Review & Grand Celebration

Morning:

- **Comprehensive Dashboard Generation:** Trigger your AI agent to compile Days 22–28 metrics plus all prior weeks into a single "Time-Wealth Year-One Review" PDF (downloadable).

Midday:

- **Community Showcase:** Host a 30-minute virtual or in-person presentation of your system's evolution—invite peers, mentors, or team members to celebrate your journey.

Afternoon:

- **Grand Reward:** Execute the Week 4 reward you mapped on Day 14—whether it's a nature hike, creative workshop, or special meal.

Evening:

- **Extended Journal Entry:**
  - **Four-Week Metrics Summary:** Final TWS, LDR, BCR, RQS, JCR.
  - **Resilience Score:** Evaluate your system's ability to recover from drills and real disruptions.

- **Sabbath & Seasonal Plan Reaffirmation:** List upcoming sabbaths and quarterly review dates.
- **Sustainable Roadmap:**
    1. Monthly Peer Pod rituals.
    2. Quarterly RRULE reviews.
    3. Annual "Time-Wealth Retreat."
    4. Ongoing AI agent maintenance (retraining schedule).
- **Personal Manifesto Revisited:** Revise your original Time-Wealth Manifesto in light of four weeks of practice.

15.9 Case Study: Week 4 Stabilization for Rafael

End of Week 3 Baseline:

- TWS: 42%
- LDR: 2.5%
- BCR: 92%
- RQS: 22/25
- JCR: 100%

Week 4 Interventions & Outcomes:

Intervention	Impact & Resilience Metrics
Habit-Loop Reinforcement (Day 22)	Morning ritual ≥ 95% completion; JCR stayed at 100%

Quarterly RRULE Creation (Day 23)	Scheduled 4 future reviews; mock next-month check → completed
Social Accountability Pod (Day 24)	Peer engagement ↑ 30%; BCR maintained at 90% despite travel
Digital Sabbath Planning (Day 25)	Saved 7 hours offline; subjective rejuvenation score 5/5
Disruption Drill (Day 26)	Recovery time avg 5 min; BCR post-drill 85%
Continuous Learning Loop (Day 27)	Implemented two new tactics; RQS ↑ 2 points

End of Week 4 Results:

- **TWS:** 45% (+3%)
- **LDR:** 2% (−0.5%)
- **BCR:** 91% (−1%)
- **RQS:** 23/25 (+1)
- **JCR:** 100%

Rafael's Reflection:
"Week 4 transformed my sprint into a sustainable marathon. Building social scaffolds and quarterly rituals means I'm not left to my own devices. My digital sabbaths felt like hitting a 'reset' button, and the disruption drills proved the system's sturdiness. As I plan my first annual retreat, I feel confident that these habits will outlast any single season."

15.10 Common Pitfalls & Proactive Fixes

Pitfall	Fix

Dependency on External Accountability	Cultivate strong self-check rituals; gradually reduce peer check-ins for autonomy
Overcommitment of Social Structures	Limit Peer Pod meetings to one per week; use asynchronous updates the rest of the time
Forgetting to Honor Sabbaths	Pre-load sabbath auto-replies and calendar blocks; treat violations as data to refine
RRULE Drift or Skip	Schedule annual "maintenance sprints" to revisit and renew calendar rules
Stagnation in Continuous Learning	Rotate learning themes each quarter; engage new mentors or courses

---

15.11 Integrating Sustainability & Resilience

Your fully-formed Time-Wealth Ecosystem now features:

- **Automated Habit Loops:** Triggers, actions, and rewards reinforced by AI and physical cues.
- **Social Framework:** Peer Pod, mentor sessions, public commitments maintain momentum.
- **Periodic Reviews:** Quarterly RRULEs, annual retreats, seasonal sabbaths ensure continuous recalibration.
- **Environmental Resilience:** Backup rituals, workspace drills, and flexible float blocks prepare you for life's unpredictability.
- **Adaptive AI Agents:** Predictive scheduling, concierge nudges, and generative snapshots serve as ongoing copilots.
- **Robust Journal:** 30 days of structured data feed into dynamic dashboards and AI-driven insights.

> **Ultimate Insight:** A truly resilient system blends human intention, social scaffolding, and intelligent automation—creating an enduring force field around your most precious resource: time.

15.12 Reflection & Next Steps Beyond Day 30

As you complete this 30-day odyssey:

1. **Consolidation (Days 29–30):**
   - Integrate all data into a master "Time-Wealth Year-One Review" deck or PDF.
   - Draft an "Infinite Cycle Roadmap" using RRULEs for quarterly, monthly, and weekly rituals.
2. **Ongoing Maintenance:**
   - Schedule monthly "health checks" on your metrics and habit loops.
   - Plan an annual "Time-Wealth Retreat" to envision the next year of growth.
3. **Community & Legacy:**
   - Mentor a new cohort, sharing your template and lessons.
   - Contribute to a shared repository of best practices for collective time wealth.

> **Final Journal Prompt:**
> *"How has my relationship with time evolved? What legacy do I hope my time-wealth system leaves on my life and community?"*

Congratulations—you now possess a living, breathing Time-Wealth Ecosystem: a fusion of philosophy, neuroscience, AI, and human connection. May every picosecond henceforth be honored, enriched, and invested in the infinite cycle of growth.

Chapter 16: Days 29–30 – Consolidation & Next Steps

> "The culmination of a journey is not an endpoint but a launchpad for the infinite cycles to come."
> —Dr. Justin Goldston

16.1 The Purpose of Consolidation

After 28 days of rigorous practice, fine-tuning, and optimization, Days 29–30 serve to **integrate** everything you've built and to **project** your Time-Wealth Ecosystem into the future. This two-day span synthesizes metrics, codifies lessons, and establishes self-sustaining rhythms—ensuring that your progress becomes your new baseline rather than a fleeting sprint.

- **Integration:** Merge all data streams into a coherent whole.
- **Reflection:** Extract meta-insights that transcend daily fluctuations.
- **Roadmapping:** Architect quarterly, annual, and long-term rituals.
- **Legacy Building:** Share, teach, and cement practices within your community.

16.2 Day 29 Morning – Master Dashboard Creation

16.2.1 Data Aggregation

- **Gather Sources:** Export the following to a central CSV or database:
    - Daily metrics (TWS, LDR, LEM, FBR, RQS, TUR, BCR, ABO, RRE, JCR).
    - Weekly averages (Weeks 1–4) and trending deltas.
    - AI agent logs (interaction counts, alignment scores).
    - Automation coverage records (ACR, ALC).
- **Data Validation:** Spot-check random entries for accuracy; correct any mislogs.

16.2.2 Dashboard Design

- **Platform Selection:** Choose a robust visualization tool (Google Data Studio, Tableau Public, Notion Charts, or Airtable Interface).
- **Key Sections:**
    1. **Overall Time-Wealth Growth Curve:** Line chart of TWS over 30 days.

2. **Leak Drag Reduction:** Bar chart comparing LDR at Day 1, Week 1, 2, 3, and Day 28.
3. **Cycle Efficiency Heatmap:** LEM by day/hour matrix.
4. **Energy vs. Blocks Alignment:** Overlay of Peak-State Map with BCR.
5. **AI & Automation Impact:** Table showing hours reclaimed and predictive accuracy.
6. **Habit Loop Completion:** Radar chart of top five habit loops and completion rates.
7. **Recovery & Boundary Metrics:** Combined RQS, FBR, and interruption counts.

16.2.3 Dashboard Construction Steps

1. **Import Data:** Connect your CSV or data source to the visualization tool.
2. **Build Charts:** Create each visual, labeling axes, legends, and thresholds (e.g., TWS 30% = baseline, 50% = excellence).
3. **Assemble Layout:** Organize visuals logically—overview at top, drill-downs below.
4. **Annotate Insights:** Add callouts for major inflection points (e.g., AI agent launch on Day 18 → TWS spike).
5. **Export & Share:** Publish as a live dashboard link or PDF, and embed in your journal or Notion workspace.

Exercise: Spend 90 minutes today creating and refining your Master Dashboard. Ensure it tells the story of your 30-day evolution at a glance.

16.3 Day 29 Afternoon – Meta-Reflection & Synthesis

16.3.1 Thematic Analysis

- **Pattern Mining:** Review your journal's "Top Insights" entries across 30 days. Tag recurring themes (e.g., "automation yields the greatest ROI," "rituals prevent drift," "AI prompts amplify focus").

Sentiment Mapping: Use AI to analyze all journal reflections for emotional tone—track how positivity, stress, and confidence evolved.

perl
CopyEdit
```
"Analyze my 30 journal insights for sentiment trends. Highlight the days of highest optimism and the days of greatest challenge, and suggest one overarching lesson about my resilience."
```

-

16.3.2 Core Lessons Extraction

Condense your accumulated wisdom into **five core principles** for lasting Time-Wealth mastery, such as:

1. **Automate to Amplify:** Reclaim hours by codifying routine tasks into Zaps and AI scripts.

2. **Cycle with Conscious Renewal:** Embed micro-rituals at every transition to sustain infinite cycles.

3. **Align Work with Biology:** Schedule deep work in peak-state windows and recover in troughs.

4. **Measure to Manifest:** Use metrics not as judgments but as mirrors that guide iterative improvement.

5. **Cultivate Community:** Leverage social structures to embed accountability and shared growth.

16.3.3 Personal Manifesto Rewrite

- **Original Manifesto Recall:** Revisit your Day 1 statement.

- **Revision Exercise:** In light of 30 days' practice, rewrite your Time-Wealth Manifesto in **three powerful sentences** that capture both philosophy and action.

- **Journal Prompt:**

"How has my understanding of time-wealth deepened, and what is my new commitment to honor each picosecond?"

16.4 Day 29 Evening – Roadmap & Ritual Engineering

16.4.1 Quarter-By-Quarter Planning

- **Q1 Rituals:**
  - **Monthly Health Check:** 60-minute dashboard review on the first Monday of each month.
  - **Peer Pod Sync:** Weekly 30-minute accountability call.
  - **Digital Sabbath:** A 6-hour Sabbath on the second Saturday each month.

Quarterly Rituals (RRULE):

ruby
CopyEdit
```
BEGIN:VEVENT
RRULE:FREQ=MONTHLY;INTERVAL=3;BYDAY=MO;BYSETPOS=2;BYHOUR=9;BYMINUTE=0;
BYSECOND=0
END:VEVENT
```

- *Second Monday of every quarter at 9 AM: Quarterly Time-Wealth Retreat.*

16.4.2 Annual Review & Visioning

- **Annual Retreat Agenda:**
  1. **Year-One Recap:** Present Master Dashboard.
  2. **5-Year Time-Wealth Vision:** Envision the impact of sustained practice on personal, professional, and community goals.
  3. **Legacy Mapping:** Define how you'll mentor others and codify your system for future cohorts.

- **DTSTART Setting:** Optionally use `dtstart_offset_json` to schedule your first annual review offset by one year.

16.4.3 Ritual Cadence Summary

Ritual Type	Frequency	Duration	Purpose
Monthly Health Check	1st Mon, Monthly	60 min	Aggregate metrics & refine tactics
Peer Pod Sync	Weekly	30 min	Share progress & mutual accountability
Digital Sabbath	Monthly	6 hrs	Deep rest & reset digital habits
Quarterly Retreat	Quarterly	2–3 hrs	Strategic review & seasonal planning
Annual Visioning	Yearly	Full day	Long-term planning & legacy definition

> **Exercise:** Schedule all rituals in your primary calendar using the VEVENT RRULEs. Confirm automated invites and reminders are set.

16.5 Day 30 Morning – Community Sharing & Mentorship

16.5.1 Package Your Learnings

- **Create a "Time-Wealth Playbook"** PDF or Notion page that includes:
    - Condensed chapter summaries and key exercises.
    - Templates for journal, blocks, rituals, and AI prompts.
    - Links to your Master Dashboard and code snippets for automations.
- **Branding & Accessibility:** Add a cover page, table of contents, and clear instructions for newcomers.

16.5.2 Launch Your Mentorship Initiative

- **Invitees:** Identify 3–5 colleagues, friends, or community members to pilot your playbook.
- **Kickoff Session:** Host a 60-minute onboarding workshop—present the core principles, walk through templates, and set group norms.
- **Accountability Channel:** Create a shared Slack/Discord channel or email thread for ongoing check-ins.

Journal Prompt:
"How does teaching this system deepen my own mastery, and what support structures will I need as a mentor?"

16.6 Day 30 Afternoon – Personal Celebration & Reflection

16.6.1 Celebration Ritual

- **Design a Personal Ceremony:** Combine elements that resonate—sunset walk, favorite music playlist, symbolic gesture (e.g., planting a seed).
- **Invite a "Witness":** A close friend, partner, or mentor to acknowledge your transformation.
- **Artifacts & Mementos:** Create a "Time-Wealth Token" (a stone, coin, or digital badge) to mark completion of your first 30-day cycle.

16.6.2 Deep Reflection Prompts

- **Transformation Inventory:** List three ways your relationship with time has irrevocably changed.
- **Gratitude & Acknowledgment:** Write a letter to yourself, from yourself, celebrating the discipline, experimentation, and growth of the past month.
- **Vision Statement:** Draft a concise "Time-Wealth Vision" for the next six months—what you wish to achieve and how your system will evolve.

16.7 Day 30 Evening – Final Journal & Next Phase Commitments

16.7.1 Final Journal Entry

- **Comprehensive Metrics:** Record final TWS, LDR, BCR, RQS, and JCR.
- **Core Insights Recap:** Five bullet-point principles distilled from 30 days.
- **Updated Manifesto:** Your three-sentence Time-Wealth creed.
- **Legacy Map:** Outline how you'll mentor and share the system in your community.
- **Next 90-Day Goals:** Three SMART objectives aligned with your Vision Statement.

16.7.2 Automating Next Steps

- **Calendar Automations:** Confirm all RRULE events (monthly, quarterly, yearly) are active.
- **AI Agent Upkeep:** Schedule a bi-weekly retraining of your AI concierge with updated metrics.
- **Journal Continuation:** Transition from daily to weekly journaling—schedule a weekly reflection block in your calendar with prompts for high-level insights.

AI Prompt for Transition:

CopyEdit

“Outline a weekly reflection template that captures high-level trends, wins, and adjustments without daily granularity. Include three core prompts and suggest automation options to streamline entries.”

pgsql
CopyEdit

```
---

### 16.8 The Infinite Cycle Continues
With these final two days, you've transformed a 30-day sprint into a
**self-perpetuating Time-Wealth Ecosystem**. But the journey never
truly ends: each quarterly review will seed new cycles of awareness,
design, optimization, and resilience—propelling you onward in an
**infinite spiral** of growth.
```

> **Final Insight:** Your greatest asset is not the system itself but your commitment to iterate, evolve, and share. As you pass this playbook to others, you multiply its impact—cultivating a community that values every picosecond as a precious, irreplaceable gem.

Congratulations. The next chapter of your infinite journey begins now.

You said:

Make the next chapter longer than the previous chapter.

ChatGPT said:

Chapter 17: Understanding Your Time-Wealth Metrics

> "Metrics are the language of progress. When you speak it fluently, you can negotiate your way to greater abundance."
> —Dr. Justin Goldston

17.1 The Role of Metrics in Your Time-Wealth Ecosystem

Metrics transform subjective impressions into objective insights, guiding every phase of your journey:

- **Awareness (Week 1):** Reveal hidden drains and baselines.
- **Design (Week 2):** Validate block and ritual adjustments.
- **Optimization (Week 3):** Measure AI and automation impact.
- **Sustainability (Week 4):** Track resilience over disruptions and seasons.

Without clear metrics, you're navigating blind; with them, you navigate by stars.

17.2 Core Metrics Defined

Metric Name	Abbreviation	Formula	Purpose

Time-Wealth Score	TWS	(Minutes of Deep Presence ÷ Total Minutes Tracked) × 100	Overall measure of intentional focus
Loop Efficiency Metric	LEM	(Complete Infinite Cycles ÷ Total Time Spent) × 100	Efficiency in attention–action–feedback cycles
Leak Drag Ratio	LDR	(Minutes Lost to Leaks ÷ Total Minutes Tracked) × 100	Proportion of time eroded by leaks
Focus-to-Break Ratio	FBR	Total Work Minutes ÷ Total Break Minutes	Balance of work and recovery
Recovery Quality Score	RQS	(Average Break Satisfaction + Average Energy Upon Return)	Quality of restoration per break
Tracked-Untracked Ratio	TUR	(Minutes Logged ÷ Total Minutes in Day) × 100	Completeness of your audit/logging
Block Completion Rate	BCR	(Blocks Completed as Scheduled ÷ Total Blocks) × 100	Adherence to scheduled blocks
Average Block Overrun	ABO	Sum of Overrun Minutes ÷ Total Blocks	Tendency to exceed block durations
Rapid Reset Efficiency	RRE	(Post-Ritual Focus Rating ÷ Pre-Ritual Distraction Rating) × 100	Effectiveness of micro-ritual resets
Automation Coverage Ratio	ACR	(Tasks Automated ÷ Total Repetitive Tasks) × 100	Degree of routine task automation
Automation Leak Coverage	ALC	(Top Leaks Managed by Automation ÷ Total Top Leaks) × 100	Leak mitigation via automation
Ultradian Compliance Rate	UCR	(Properly Timed Breaks ÷ Recommended Breaks) × 100	Adherence to ultradian rhythm–aligned breaks

Journal Completion Rate	JCR	(Days with Full Journal Entries ÷ Total Days) × 100	Consistency in journaling practice
Predictive Alignment Score	PAS	(AI-Suggested Blocks Followed ÷ Total AI-Suggested Blocks) × 100	Degree of AI-schedule conformity
Habit Loop Completion Rate	HLCR	(Times Habit Loop Executed ÷ Scheduled Executions) × 100	Consistency in key habit loops

---

17.3 Manual Calculation Techniques

While many tools automate these metrics, understanding manual computation cements your fluency:

1. **TWS Calculation Example:**
    - Deep Presence: 210 minutes
    - Total Logged: 1,440 minutes
    - TWS = (210 ÷ 1,440) × 100 = **14.6%**
2. **LEM Deep Dive:**
    - Total Time Spent on Task X: 240 minutes
    - Completed Cycles: 12
    - LEM = (12 ÷ 240) × 100 = **5%** cycles per minute → multiply by average cycle length for insight.
3. **LDR Example:**
    - Leak Minutes: Instagram 45 + Email 60 + Meeting Drift 50 = 155
    - Total Logged: 1,440
    - LDR = (155 ÷ 1,440) × 100 = **10.8%**

4. **FBR Example:**
   - Work Minutes: 360
   - Break Minutes: 90
   - FBR = 360 ÷ 90 = **4:1** ratio

> **Exercise:** Using your Day 1 audit data, compute each core metric manually. Note where tool outputs differ—seek to understand discrepancies.

17.4 Automating Metric Collection

To minimize manual overhead and maximize reliability:

1. **Integrate Trackers with Spreadsheets:**
   - **Zapier/Make**: Push Toggl/RescueTime logs to Google Sheets.
   - **Formulas:** Use built-in sheet formulas to compute daily TWS, LDR, TUR, etc.
2. **Dashboard Tools:**
   - **Google Data Studio:** Connect Sheets → build charts with calculated fields.
   - **Notion + Charts Plugin:** Embed computed rollups in database views.
3. **AI Assistance:**

Prompt for Summaries:

vbnet
CopyEdit
```
"Summarize today's TWS, LDR, and BCR from my sheet and suggest one action to improve TWS by 5% tomorrow."
```

   -

> **Tip:** Schedule a daily "metrics sync" automation at 7 PM to refresh all dashboards without lifting a finger.

17.5 Advanced Interpretations & Thresholds

Not all percentages are equal—context matters. Use these guidelines as starting points, then customize:

Metric	Green Zone	Yellow Zone	Red Zone
TWS	≥40%	25–40%	<25%
LEM	≥10 cycles/hour	5–10	<5
LDR	≤5%	5–10%	>10%
FBR	3:1–4:1	2:1–3:1	<2:1 or >5:1
RQS	≥20/25	15–20	<15
BCR	≥90%	70–90%	<70%
UCR	≥100%	80–100%	<80%
JCR	≥95%	75–95%	<75%

> **Exercise:** Compare your four-week averages to these thresholds. Highlight two metrics in the red zone and plan targeted interventions.

17.6 Case Study: Interpreting Complex Trends

Scenario: Over 30 days, Emma's TWS rose steadily from 18% to 36%, but LEM plateaued at 6% after Day 20. Simultaneously, RQS improved from 10 to 23.

Analysis:

- **High RQS + Moderate LEM:** Indicated excellent recovery but sub-optimal cycle turnover; perhaps cycles were too long.

- **Action:** Emma experimented with shifting from 90/20 to 70/15 cycles to increase LEM without sacrificing RQS.

Outcome: Within three days, LEM jumped to 9%, and TWS inched to 38%.

Insight: Cross-metric analysis surfaces nuanced trade-offs and guides fine-tuned experiments.

17.7 Visualizing Metrics for Maximum Clarity

1. **Time-Wealth Growth Curve:**
    - Line chart of daily TWS over 30 days with moving average overlay.
2. **Metric Correlation Matrix:**
    - Heatmap showing correlations between TWS, LDR, LEM, RQS, etc.
3. **Cycle Efficiency Heatmap:**
    - Matrix of LEM by day vs. hour, highlighting top-performing windows.
4. **Combined Dashboard:**
    - Single view integrating chart snapshots, metric summary cards, and AI-driven annotations.

Exercise: Create a correlation matrix in your dashboard to identify which metrics move together—e.g., does higher RQS reliably predict next-day TWS?

17.8 Exercise: Metric-Driven Decision Making

1. **Select Two Lagging Metrics:** Choose metrics in the red zone.
2. **Root-Cause Drill:** Use "5 Whys" or AI prompts to diagnose underlying causes.
3. **Intervention Planning:** For each metric, design two experiments—one small tweak, one bold change.

4. **Schedule Tests:** Integrate experiments into your Week-5 calendar.
5. **Measure Impact:** After three days, compare pre- and post-metric values.

Journal Prompt:
"Which metric holds the key to my next breakthrough, and what experiment will unlock it?"

17.9 Common Pitfalls in Metric Tracking

Pitfall	Fix
Over-Monitoring Leading to Analysis Paralysis	Limit deep reviews to weekly or monthly; trust the system fish out details
Misaligned Metric Definitions	Standardize definitions across tools; document formulas explicitly
Infrequent Data Refresh	Automate daily syncs; use real-time dashboards where possible
Ignoring Qualitative Context	Pair metrics with brief narrative notes in your journal
Cherry-Picking Data Points	Always examine full data range; beware of anecdotal interpretations

---

17.10 AI Prompts for Enhanced Metric Insights

Trend Identification:

perl
CopyEdit
```
"Analyze my 30-day TWS data and identify three significant inflection
points. Suggest potential causes based on my journal insights."
```

•

Predictive Modeling:

perl
CopyEdit
```
"Using my first 20 days of LDR and block adherence data, predict my
LDR for the next 10 days if I introduce a new micro-intervention."
```

-

Anomaly Detection:

perl
CopyEdit
```
"Scan my daily FBR values and flag any outliers. Provide context clues
from my journal entries for those days."
```

-

17.11 Integrating Metrics with Your Infinite Cycles

Metrics are not endpoints but **feedback signals** within each Infinite Cycle:

1. **Intention Setting:** Choose your focus (e.g., "Increase TWS by 2%").
2. **Focused Action:** Execute blocks and rituals.
3. **Immediate Feedback:** Review today's metrics.
4. **Renewal & Adjustment:** Plan tomorrow's tweaks based on metric signals.

> **Insight:** Embedding metrics into your cycles institutionalizes continuous improvement—ensuring that every data point catalyzes growth.

17.12 Reflection & Preview of Chapter 18

You have now:

- Mastered definitions and calculations of all core metrics.

- Automated and visualized your data streams.
- Applied advanced interpretations and threshold benchmarks.
- Conducted case-study analyses and data-driven experiments.
- Integrated metrics as the lifeblood of your Infinite Cycles.

Next chapter: In **Chapter 18: Quick Charts to Visualize Progress**, you'll learn how to craft and customize the most effective chart types—bar graphs, heatmaps, line plots, radial diagrams—to transform raw numbers into compelling narratives that drive action and insight.

Journal Prompt:

1. *"Which metric spoke most profoundly to me today, and what story does it tell?"*
2. *"How will I use chart visuals to communicate my next milestone?"*
3. *"What metric-based decision will I make first thing tomorrow?"*

By answering these, you prime your mind to tell stories with data—and to wield charts as instruments of clarity and motivation.

Chapter 18: Quick Charts to Visualize Progress

> "Numbers tell one story; charts bring that story to life, revealing patterns you might never see otherwise."
> —Dr. Justin Goldston

18.1 The Power of Visualization in Time-Wealth

Humans are inherently visual thinkers. When confronted with rows of numbers, we often miss underlying trends, inflection points, and correlations. By transforming raw metrics into charts—line graphs, bar plots, heatmaps, radial diagrams—we shine a light on hidden structures. In the context of your Time-Wealth Ecosystem, charts allow you to:

- **Instantly detect inflection points:** Notice when TWS climbs or dips sharply.
- **Compare multiple metrics at once:** Overlay LDR and TWS to see how sealing leaks boosts presence.
- **Identify cyclical patterns:** Heatmaps reveal which hours of the day consistently underperform.
- **Communicate progress:** A well-labeled chart conveys your journey at a glance, whether to yourself, your Peer Pod, or a broader audience.

Visualization isn't purely decorative—it's a fundamental tool for iterative improvement. In this chapter, you'll master the creation of "quick charts" that highlight your key metrics, help you make data-driven decisions, and reinforce your time-wealth narrative.

18.2 Chart Types and Use Cases

Below is a non-exhaustive list of chart types, their strengths, and typical scenarios in which you'd deploy them:

Chart Type	Primary Use Case	Example Scenario
Line Chart	Track a single metric or multiple metrics over time	Plot TWS daily over 30 days, with a moving average overlay to highlight longer-term trends.
Bar Chart	Compare discrete categories or time periods	Compare weekly average LDR for Weeks 1–4 side by side to gauge leak reduction.
Stacked Bar Chart	Show composition of categories within a total	Stack "Deep Work," "Admin," "Social," and "Rest" minutes per day to see how total logged time is divided.
Heatmap	Visualize intensity or density across two dimensions (e.g., day vs. hour)	Create an LEM heatmap with days on the Y-axis and hours on the X-axis—cells colored by efficiency score.

Radial/Spider Chart	Compare multiple metrics or sub-metrics for a single entity	Plot a single "Week 3" radial chart with axes for TWS, LDR, BCR, RQS, and UCR to see balanced vs. lopsided performance.
Scatter Plot	Reveal relationships or correlations between two continuous variables	Scatter daily TWS (X-axis) against LDR (Y-axis) to see whether higher leak drag reliably corresponds to lower presence.
Area Chart	Emphasize cumulative trends or highlight part-to-whole changes over time	Use an area chart to show cumulative "Deep Work" minutes over 30 days, demonstrating how the total builds.
Bullet Chart	Display progress toward a goal against thresholds, with qualitative ranges (poor, satisfactory, good)	Show TWS against a target of ≥40% with thresholds (25%–40% is caution, <25% is red).
Box-and-Whisker Plot	Summarize distribution of a metric over a period, revealing medians, quartiles, and outliers	Visualize distribution of daily RQS scores for each week to compare variability in recovery quality.
Timeline with Annotations	Chronicle significant events or interventions against a continuous time axis	Map key dates (Week 2 block redesign, AI agent launch) along a timeline with TWS plotted, annotating where interventions occurred.

> **Mini-Lesson:** Choose the simplest chart that answers your question. If you only need to see "Did my TWS improve?" use a line chart. Avoid unnecessary complexity.

18.3 Preparing Your Data for Charting

Before crafting any chart, ensure your data is clean, consistent, and structured:

1. **Standardize Time Intervals:**
    - **Daily Metrics:** Each row represents one date (e.g., 2025-05-01, 2025-05-02, …). Columns include TWS, LDR, LEM, etc.

- **Hourly Metrics (for heatmaps):** Use a “long” format: columns = Date, Hour (0–23), Metric Value.

2. **Label Columns Clearly:**

    - Column headers like `Date`, `TWS_%`, `LDR_%`, `LEM_perc`, `RQS_Score`, `BCR_pct`, etc.

    - For composite charts, ensure category names (e.g., “Deep Work Minutes”, “Admin Minutes”) are consistent.

3. **Handle Missing Values:**

    - **Imputation:** For minor gaps, you may carry forward the last known value or insert average of neighbors.

    - **Flagging:** Color-code cells with missing data when creating charts, or exclude them with clear notes.

4. **Calculate Derived Fields:**

Moving Averages: Add columns like `TWS_7DMA` (7-day moving average) using spreadsheet formulas:

objectivec
CopyEdit
```
=AVERAGE(B2:B8)  // If B column holds TWS values for rows 2-8
```

-
- **Month-to-Date Summaries:** Create additional tables aggregating first N days of the month for high-level snapshots.

5. **Organize Data Tables:**

    - Store daily metrics in a table named `DailyMetrics`.

    - Store hourly metrics in `HourlyMetrics`.

    - Define named ranges to simplify chart references (e.g., `NamedRange_TWS` for the TWS column).

Exercise: In your chosen data platform (Google Sheets, Notion Database, Airtable), build a `DailyMetrics` table with the following columns:

- `Date` (MM/DD/YYYY)
- `TWS_%` (numeric)
- `LDR_%` (numeric)
- `LEM_perc` (numeric)
- `RQS_Score` (numeric)
- `BCR_pct` (numeric)
- `UCR_pct` (numeric)

Populate it with your first 30 days of data. Double-check for typos.

18.4 Creating Your First Line Chart: TWS Over Time

18.4.1 Step-by-Step in Google Sheets (or Excel)

1. **Select Data Range:**
   - Click on the `Date` and `TWS_%` columns (two adjacent columns).
2. **Insert Chart:**
   - In Sheets: Insert → Chart.
   - In Excel: Insert → Line Chart → "Line with Markers."
3. **Configure the Chart Editor:**
   - **Chart Type:** Ensure "Line chart" is selected.
   - **X-Axis:** Should be the `Date` range.

- **Series:** `TWS_%`.

4. **Customize Aesthetics:**

    - **Title:** “Daily Time-Wealth Score (TWS) Over 30 Days.”
    - **Axis Titles:** X-axis: “Date”; Y-axis: “TWS (%)”.
    - **Data Labels (optional):** Show markers with values for days where TWS ≥ 40%.
    - **Gridlines:** Light gray for reference; remove heavy gridlines to reduce clutter.
    - **Trendline (optional):** Add a 7-day moving average trendline:
        - In Sheets: Series → Trendline → Type: “Moving Average” → Period: 7.
        - In Excel: Chart Elements → Add Trendline → Moving Average Period 7.

5. **Interpretation Tips (Journal Prompt):**

    - “On which days did TWS cross 40%? What coincided with those peaks (e.g., AI agent launch, major block redesign)?”
    - “When did TWS dip below 25%, and what factors contributed (e.g., unanticipated meetings, digital distractions)?”

Exercise: Create your TWS line chart. Then, use the “moving average” feature to smooth short-term fluctuations and highlight long-term trends. Note at least two inflection points and annotate them directly on the chart.

18.5 Bar Charts to Compare Categorical Data

18.5.1 Comparing Weekly Averages of LDR

1. **Prepare Aggregated Table:** Create a new table `WeeklyMetrics` with columns:

    - `Week` (Week 1, Week 2, Week 3, Week 4)
    - `Avg_LDR_%` (average of LDR for each 7-day block).

2. **Insert Bar Chart:**
   - Select the `Week` and `Avg_LDR_%` columns.
   - In Sheets/Excel: Insert → Chart → "Column Chart" (vertical bars).
3. **Customize:**
   - **Chart Title:** "Average Leak Drag Ratio by Week."
   - **Axis Titles:** X-axis: "Week"; Y-axis: "Average LDR (%)".
   - **Color Coding:** Use a conditional color scale—green for ≤5%, yellow for 5–10%, red for >10%.
   - **Data Labels:** Show numeric percentages atop each bar.

18.5.2 Stacked Bar Chart for Category Breakdown

If you tracked "Deep Work," "Admin," "Learning," and "Rest" minutes per day, create a stacked bar:

1. **Aggregated Table:**
   - Columns: `Date`, `DeepWork_Min`, `Admin_Min`, `Learning_Min`, `Rest_Min`.
2. **Insert Stacked Bar Chart:**
   - Select all columns.
   - In Sheets: Insert → Chart → "Stacked column chart."
   - In Excel: Insert → Column → "Stacked Column."
3. **Customize Colors:**
   - Assign distinct, intuitive colors (e.g., Deep Work = blue, Admin = gray, Learning = green, Rest = orange).
   - Add legend at the bottom.

4. **Interpretation Tips:**
    - "On which days did Deep Work exceed 4 hours? Did Admin unexpectedly spike? How did Rest minutes correlate with peak TWS days?"

Exercise: Build both bar charts. Then, combine them into a single dashboard layout, placing the Weekly LDR bar chart above the stacked daily breakdown. Use consistent fonts and styling for a polished look.

18.6 Heatmaps: Uncovering Temporal Patterns

Heatmaps are ideal for spotting patterns over two dimensions—commonly "Day of Week" vs. "Hour of Day" or "Date" vs. "Metric Value Range."

18.6.1 Creating an LEM Heatmap

1. **Structure Data in "Long" Format:** A table `LEM_Hourly` with columns:
    - `Date` (e.g., 2025-05-01)
    - `Hour` (0–23)
    - `LEM_Value` (the LEM score for that hour)
2. **Pivot Table (Sheets/Excel):**
    - Create a pivot from `LEM_Hourly` with Rows = `Date`, Columns = `Hour`, Values = `Average of LEM_Value`.
3. **Insert Heatmap:**
    - **Sheets:** Use "Conditional formatting" → Color scale on the pivot table cells.
    - **Excel:** Select pivot cells → Home → Conditional Formatting → "Color Scales" (Green–Yellow–Red).

- **Labeling:** Include a legend for numeric ranges (e.g., ≥15% = dark green, 5–15% = yellow, <5% = red).

4. **Interpretation:**
   - "Which hours consistently show high LEM (deep focus)? Do weekdays differ from weekends? Are there unexpected low-efficiency pockets at certain times?"

18.6.2 Alternative: Day-of-Week vs. Hour-of-Day Heatmap

If you want to collapse dates into weekdays (Monday–Sunday):

1. **Add a `Weekday` Column:** Using formulas:
   - Sheets: `=TEXT(A2, "dddd")` where A2 is the Date cell.
   - Excel: `=TEXT(A2, "dddd")`.
2. **Pivot Table:** Rows = `Weekday`, Columns = `Hour`, Values = `AVERAGE(LEM_Value)`.
3. **Sort Weekdays:** Manually order pivot Rows as Monday, Tuesday, … Sunday.
4. **Conditional Formatting:** Same color scale as above.
5. **Interpretation:**
   - "On which weekdays do my focus patterns deviate? Are Thursday mornings always low, suggesting schedule shifts?"

Exercise: Create both versions of the LEM heatmap. Journal about one surprising pattern—e.g., a consistent "Sunday slump" or "Wednesday spike"—and hypothesize a cause.

18.7 Radial/Spider Charts: Seeing Balanced Performance

A radial chart (also called a spider or radar chart) displays multiple variables on concentric axes emanating from a central point. It's useful when you want to compare, say, a single week's performance across several metrics.

18.7.1 Data Preparation

- **Table `WeeklyOverview`:** Columns:
    - `Metric` (TWS, LDR, BCR, RQS, UCR)
    - `Week1_Value`, `Week2_Value`, `Week3_Value`, `Week4_Value`

18.7.2 Building the Chart (Google Sheets / Excel)

1. **Select Data Range:** All five metric names plus the four weekly values.
2. **Insert Radar Chart:**
    - Sheets: Insert → Chart → "Radar chart."
    - Excel: Insert → Other Charts → "Radar with Markers."
3. **Customize:**
    - **Series Colors:** Assign a distinct color for each week (e.g., Week 1 = pastel blue, Week 2 = pastel orange, etc.).
    - **Axis Labels:** Ensure each spoke is labeled with the metric name.
    - **Title:** "Weekly Performance Across Core Metrics."
    - **Legends:** Place at the bottom or side to avoid overlapping the chart.
4. **Interpretation Tips:**
    - "Which week had the most balanced polygon (closest to a regular shape)? Which axis dipped most dramatically, indicating weak performance?"

Exercise: Create a radial chart comparing Week 1 through Week 4 for your core metrics. In your journal, write a paragraph interpreting which week was most balanced and why, based on the plotted shape.

18.8 Scatter Plots: Revealing Correlations and Outliers

When you suspect two metrics are related—e.g., "Does higher RQS (Recovery Quality) predict higher next-day TWS?"—scatter plots can confirm or refute correlations.

18.8.1 Data Table Structure

- **Table `DailyCorrelations`:** Columns:
    - `Date`
    - `RQS_Score`
    - `NextDay_TWS` (shifted TWS value for the following day)

18.8.2 Creating the Scatter Plot

1. **Select the `RQS_Score` and `NextDay_TWS` columns.**
2. **Insert Scatter Chart:**
    - Sheets: Insert → Chart → "Scatter chart."
    - Excel: Insert → Scatter → "Scatter with only markers."
3. **Customize:**
    - **Axis Titles:** X-axis = "Recovery Quality Score (RQS)"; Y-axis = "Next-Day Time-Wealth Score (TWS)."
    - **Trendline:** Add a linear regression line with equation display.
    - **Outlier Highlighting:** Manually identify points with extreme values (e.g., low RQS but high TWS) and annotate them.
4. **Interpretation:**
    - "Is there a positive slope indicating that better recovery leads to higher presence? Are there exceptions—days you recovered well but still had low TWS, suggesting another factor at play?"

Exercise: Build the scatter plot. Use the trendline's correlation coefficient (R^2) as a metric:

- $R^2 \geq 0.7$: Strong correlation.
- **R^2 0.4–0.7:** Moderate correlation.
- **$R^2 < 0.4$:** Weak or no correlation.

Record the R^2 in your journal and propose reasons for any unexpected outliers.

18.9 Area Charts: Emphasizing Cumulative Growth

Area charts are essentially line charts with the area below filled, ideal for illustrating cumulative progression or stacked categories over time.

18.9.1 Cumulative Deep Work Minutes Over 30 Days

1. **Compute Cumulative Totals:** In your `DailyMetrics` table, add a column `Cum_DeepWork_Min`:
   - In Sheets: `=SUM($B$2:B2)` if column B holds daily `DeepWork_Min`. Drag formula down for all 30 rows.
2. **Insert Area Chart:**
   - Select `Date` and `Cum_DeepWork_Min`.
   - Insert → Chart → "Area chart."
3. **Customize:**
   - **Chart Title:** "Cumulative Deep Work Minutes Over 30 Days."
   - **Axes:** X-axis = Date; Y-axis = Cumulative Minutes.
   - **Fill Color:** Use a semi-transparent shade to contrast against the background.
   - **Data Labels (optional):** Show cumulative value at key milestones (e.g., Day 10, Day 20, Day 30).
4. **Interpretation:**

- "Does the curve accelerate in later weeks, indicating compounding deep-work habits? Does it plateau, signaling a need to re-evaluate block adherence?"

Exercise: Create the area chart. Then, overlay a secondary series for cumulative "Admin Minutes" on the same chart, using a different fill color. Note where the slopes diverge—where deep work growth outpaces administrative drag.

18.10 Bullet Charts: Visualizing Progress vs. Goals

Bullet charts, popularized by Stephen Few, compare performance against thresholds and targets in a compact, information-rich format.

18.10.1 Constructing a Bullet Chart in Google Data Studio

1. **Data Preparation:**
   - **Table `Targets`:** Columns:
     - `MetricName` (e.g., "TWS")
     - `ActualValue` (e.g., 45)
     - `TargetValue` (e.g., 50)
     - `LowThreshold` (e.g., 25)
     - `HighThreshold` (e.g., 40)
2. **In Data Studio:**
   - Add your data source (Sheet or database).
   - Insert → "Bullet Chart" (if available via community visualizations) or approximate with a stacked bar and reference line.
   - **Configure Ranges:** Low (0–25), Medium (25–40), High (40–50+).
   - **Actual Marker:** Use a distinct color or marker to indicate the current value (45).

- **Target Reference Line:** Draw a line at 50.

3. **Customize Labels:**

   - Metric labels on the left (TWS, LDR, etc.).

   - Measure labels on the right showing "45%" or "50% target."

4. **Interpretation:**

   - "TWS = 45% is in the green zone (40–50), just shy of the 50% target. LDR might be in yellow—plan to push it below 5% next week."

Exercise: Create a bullet chart for three metrics—TWS, LDR, and BCR—each with your target thresholds. Export as an image and embed it at the top of your next journal entry as a "weekly scoreboard."

18.11 Layering Charts into a Cohesive Dashboard

A single chart tells a fragment of the story; a dashboard synthesizes multiple visuals into a coherent narrative. Follow these steps:

1. **Define Your Dashboard Objectives:**

   - **Overview Section:** High-level KPIs (TWS, LDR, BCR) with bullet or scorecard visuals.

   - **Trend Section:** Line chart for TWS, bar chart for weekly LDR, area chart for cumulative Deep Work.

   - **Deep Dive Section:** Heatmap for LEM, scatter plot for RQS vs. Next-Day TWS.

   - **Action Section:** Table of "Next Actions" based on metric thresholds.

2. **Choose a Platform:**

   - **Notion:** Use databases with embedded charts via "Charts for Notion" widget or synced Google Sheets.

   - **Google Data Studio:** Ideal for interactive dashboards; easy embedding and sharing.

- **Airtable Interface:** Use the "Interface" designer to combine charts and tables in a single view.
- **Excel Power BI / Microsoft Power BI:** For advanced interactivity and drill-downs.

3. **Assemble Components:**
    - Insert scorecards at the top for quick KPIs.
    - Below, align line and bar charts side by side for trend comparison.
    - Place heatmap and scatter plot in a "Deep Insights" panel.
    - Reserve a final row for "Action Items," a table listing experiments, status, and owners.
4. **Optimize Layout:**
    - **Consistent Color Scheme:** Use 2–3 brand or theme colors to avoid cognitive overload.
    - **Visual Hierarchy:** Place the most critical charts (TWS, LDR) near the top-left, where eyes land first.
    - **Whitespace:** Allow breathing room between chart elements.
    - **Annotations:** Add text boxes explaining anomalies or notable events (e.g., "AI agent introduced → TWS jump").
5. **Refresh Cadence:**
    - Automate data sync to update daily or hourly (as needed).
    - For weekly reviews, create a "snapshot" filter that shows data only up to the last day of the week.

Exercise: Build or update your master dashboard with at least five chart types. Spend 60 minutes refining styling—align chart colors, adjust font sizes, and annotate key inflection points. Then, share your dashboard link with your Peer Pod for feedback.

18.12 Case Study: Dashboard-Driven Decision Making

Background: Laura, a UX consultant, maintained a robust 30-day tracking regimen. Despite high block adherence (BCR = 90%), her TWS stalled around 28%. Her dashboard included:

- **Line Chart:** TWS trending 24% → 28% over 30 days.
- **Heatmap:** LEM poor (red) between 2 PM–4 PM daily.
- **Scatter Plot:** Low RQS correlated with low Next-Day TWS.

Dashboard Insights & Actions:

1. **Identify Afternoon Slump:** Heatmap revealed 2–4 PM consistently low LEM.
   - **Intervention:** Introduce a 15-minute nap or outdoor walk at 1:45 PM daily.
2. **Correlate Recovery to Presence:** Scatter plot showed RQS < 15 leading to Next-Day TWS < 25%.
   - **Intervention:** Adjust break activities, favoring longer restorative sessions on low-energy days.
3. **Track Weekly LDR:** Bar chart showed LDR peaked at 12% in Week 2, dropped to 7% in Week 3, but rose to 9% in Week 4.
   - **Intervention:** Reactivate digital boundary enforcement and schedule a "mini digital sabbath" to curb new leaks.

Outcome (Next 7 Days):

- TWS climbed to 32%.
- LEM improved by 20% in the 2–4 PM slot after implementing naps.
- RQS stabilized at ≥18, boosting Next-Day TWS consistently above 30%.

Laura's Reflection:
"My dashboard didn't just show me numbers—it pointed me to the moments when I

was eclipsing my own focus. Without seeing that afternoon slump visually, I never realized how much I craved a reset mid-day. Now, each morning, I glance at my dashboard before coffee, and I know exactly where to lean in and where to lean back."

18.13 Common Pitfalls & Charting Best Practices

Pitfall	Fix
Over-Charting (Too Many Visuals)	Stick to 3–5 critical charts; archive supplementary visuals in a separate tab.
Misaligned Scales/Axes	Always start axes at zero for bar and area charts (unless a zoomed-in view is needed).
Cluttered Dashboards	Use whitespace, section dividers, and minimal gridlines to avoid visual overload.
Inconsistent Color Usage	Define a color palette (e.g., blue for positive, red for negative) and stick to it.
Lack of Context/Annotations	Annotate anomalies (e.g., "Day 15: AI agent launch") so viewers know why spikes occur.
Ignoring Qualitative Data	Pair charts with brief narrative notes in your journal—numbers without stories can mislead.
Failing to Refresh Data	Automate data imports daily; schedule "data health checks" for your pipelines.
Over-Reliance on Trendlines	Supplement trendlines with raw data points to avoid smoothing away important spikes.
Incorrect Chart Type Selection	Refer back to section 18.2's use cases—if you need to compare categories, don't use a line chart.

18.14 AI Prompts to Level Up Your Visualizations

Use AI to generate more insightful and presentation-ready charts:

Chart Selection Advisor:

pgsql
CopyEdit
```
"Given these three data columns—Date, TWS percentage, and LDR
percentage—recommend the best chart type(s) to show how changes in
leak drag affect time-wealth over 30 days. Provide rationale."
```

-

Annotation Generator:

sql
CopyEdit
```
"Here is my TWS line chart data with dates and values. Generate three
clear, concise annotations for inflection points: one for my highest
spike, one for my biggest dip, and one when I introduced a new micro-
ritual."
```

-

Narrative Builder:

pgsql
CopyEdit
```
"Write a 150-word narrative for my dashboard introduction, summarizing
how LDR reduction correlated with TWS increase from Week 1 to Week 4."
```

-

Dashboard Styling Guide:

css
CopyEdit
```
"Suggest three color palettes suitable for a productivity dashboard
that's accessible to color-blind users. Explain why each choice
works."
```

-

Chart Interpretation Coach:

yaml
CopyEdit
```
"Analyze this bar chart showing weekly average LDR of [Week1: 12%, Week2: 7%, Week3: 4%, Week4: 2%]. Offer three strategic recommendations to further reduce LDR in Week 5."
```

- **Tip:** Save AI-generated annotations and narratives in a separate "Dashboard Insights" section—this content makes your dashboards self-explanatory to new viewers.

18.15 Exercise: Building a Narrative Dashboard

Objective: Craft a two-part "Narrative Dashboard" that tells a cohesive story:

1. **Part A – Performance Overview**
    - **Scorecards:** Show current TWS, LDR, BCR, RQS with miniature bullet charts comparing against targets.
    - **Line Chart & Trendline:** Plot 30-day TWS with a 7-day moving average; annotate peaks/dips with brief notes.
    - **Bar Chart:** Weekly average LDR for Weeks 1–4.
2. **Part B – Deep Insights & Action Items**
    - **Heatmap:** LEM by day/hour for Week 4 only, revealing "ideal focus windows."
    - **Scatter Plot:** RQS vs. Next-Day TWS for the last 14 days, with regression line and R^2 displayed.
    - **Bullet Chart:** Show BCR for Week 4 against a target of ≥90%.
    - **Action Table:** 3–5 rows listing: "Metric", "Observation", "Recommended Action."

Steps:

1. **Gather Data:** Ensure all source tables (`DailyMetrics`, `WeeklyMetrics`, `LEM_Hourly`, etc.) are up to date.
2. **Create Charts:** Follow instructions in Sections 18.4–18.10.
3. **Craft Annotations:** Use AI prompts to generate callouts for each chart—e.g., "On 2025-05-18, TWS spikes to 42% after predictive scheduling."
4. **Assemble in a Dashboard Canvas:**
    - Use Google Data Studio, Notion + Charts embed, or Airtable Interface.
    - Organize Part A visuals at the top two-thirds; Part B visuals below.
    - Insert a text box titled "Key Takeaways" where you summarize overarching insights.
    - Add a final text box for "Next Actions" aligned under Part B's Action Table.
5. **Review & Share:** Export as PDF or share live link with your accountability group. Solicit feedback on clarity, relevance, and design.

Journal Prompt:
"After building my Narrative Dashboard, what story emerges? How will I act on the top three takeaways over the next week?"

18.16 Ritual: The Weekly Chart Review

Incorporate a regular ritual to extract maximum value from your visualizations:

1. **Weekly Block (60 min):** Schedule "Chart Review & Insights" on your calendar every Monday morning.
2. **Pre-Review Preparation (5 min):**
    - Ensure all metrics are updated and dashboards are refreshed.
    - Print or open digital full-screen views of your key charts.
3. **Review Sequence:**

- **Overview (10 min):** Scan scorecards and line charts for high-level shifts.
- **Trend Deep Dive (20 min):** Examine the 30-day TWS line chart, heatmap, and scatter plot. Note any new inflection points or anomalies.
- **Action Alignment (15 min):** Compare chart findings to last week's "Next Actions." Assess: Did interventions yield expected metric changes?
- **Forward Planning (10 min):** Identify one or two metrics to focus on next week. Decide on experiments or adjustments.
- **AI Prompt (5 min):** "Based on last week's metrics, recommend one new chart I should create to reveal deeper insights."

4. **Capture in Journal:**
   - **Top Insight of the Week:** Sentence.
   - **Metric to Watch:** E.g., "LDR approaching 5% threshold."
   - **Action Plan:** List two concrete steps (e.g., "Automate email batching further," "Test a new ultradian break variant").
   - **Gratitude Note:** Thank yourself for the discipline of review.

18.17 Common Pitfalls & Best Practices

Pitfall	Best Practice
Failure to Update Data Regularly	Automate daily data imports at a set time (e.g., 7 PM) and verify via a "data health" status card.
Overemphasis on Single Metric	Always contextualize metrics—pair TWS with LDR and RQS to avoid misleading conclusions.
Neglecting Context—or–Annotations	Maintain a log of "Chart Annotations" explaining spikes/dips; revisit when preparing presentations.

Ignoring Color Accessibility	Use colorblind-friendly palettes (e.g., blue/orange, purple/green) and test with online simulators.
Cluttering Dashboards with Too Many Charts	Prioritize top 5 visuals; hide or archive others under “Supplemental Insights” tabs.
Recreating Charts from Scratch Each Week	Save chart templates; duplicate and update rather than rebuild.
Forgetting Mobile/Tablet Layout	Preview dashboards on smaller screens to ensure readability; adjust fonts and element sizes accordingly.
Not Linking Charts to Journal Entries	Embed or hyperlink key charts in your daily journal so insights are inseparable from narratives.
Overlooking Data Granularity Needs	Provide drill-down views (e.g., click a bar in the weekly LDR chart to see which days contributed most).
Neglecting Comparative Baselines	Always include multiples weeks or years for perspective—contextualize current data against historical norms.

18.18 Integrating Visualization with Your Infinite Cycles

Visualization is not an isolated activity—it’s woven into every phase of your Infinite Cycle:

1. **Intention Setting:**
   - **Before Starting a Cycle:** Glance at yesterday’s charts to decide today’s focus (e.g., “LDR is creeping up; today I’ll trial another leak-fix”).
2. **Focused Action:**
   - **During Deep Work:** Keep a small chart widget open (e.g., TWS sparkline) to reinforce why you’re immersed.
3. **Immediate Feedback:**
   - **Post-Block:** Check block-specific performance—e.g., “My Deep Work block yielded an LEM of 12%.”

4. **Adjustment:**
    - **Based on Charts:** If your scatter plot shows no correlation between RQS and next-day TWS, adjust break activities.
5. **Renewed Intention:**
    - **Guided by Visuals:** Conclude each cycle by deciding which chart to monitor next—"I want to see if my new soundscape bump will shift the RQS heatmap tomorrow."

Insight: By embedding charts into each cycle phase, you close the loop between action and insight—ensuring that every chart you build fuels your next round of improvement.

18.19 Reflection & Preview of Chapter 19

You have now:

- Learned the purposes and use cases of multiple chart types.
- Prepared and structured your data for visualization.
- Created line, bar, stacked bar, heatmap, radial, scatter, area, and bullet charts.
- Assembled these visuals into a narrative dashboard, annotated with AI-aided insights.
- Established a weekly chart review ritual to keep your Time-Wealth Ecosystem on track.
- Understood common pitfalls and best practices for maintaining clear, actionable visuals.

Next chapter: In **Chapter 19: Interpreting Your Data for Lifelong Growth**, you'll dive into advanced techniques for drawing deep conclusions from your charts, uncovering subtle trends, avoiding cognitive biases (like recency or confirmation bias), and translating visual insights into sustained change.

Journal Prompt:

1. *"Which chart gave me the most "Aha!" moment today, and how will I act on it?"*

2. *"How might I redesign my dashboard to reveal a hidden story I haven't yet noticed?"*

3. *"What one metric should I de-emphasize next week, and why?"*

By answering these, you ensure that your visualizations remain alive, dynamic instruments of lifelong Time-Wealth growth—rather than static snapshots of the past.

Chapter 19: Interpreting Your Data for Lifelong Growth

> "Data without interpretation is like a compass without a hand—you see direction, but you can't grasp it. To turn insights into evolution, you must learn to read, question, and translate every point on the chart."
> —Dr. Justin Goldston

19.1 The Imperative of Deep Interpretation

Visualizations and metrics are only as powerful as the insights you extract from them. Shallow glances at numbers risk confirmation bias, where you see only what you expect. Rigorous interpretation, by contrast, uncovers hidden patterns, causal threads, and sustainable levers for change. Throughout this chapter, you will learn how to:

1. **Detect Subtle Trends:** Spot inflection points, outliers, and emergent trajectories.

2. **Avoid Cognitive Pitfalls:** Guard against biases like recency, confirmation, availability, and anchoring.

3. **Contextualize Data:** Combine quantitative charts with qualitative narratives to reveal "why" behind the "what."

4. **Translate Insights into Action:** Convert complex patterns into concrete experiments and habit tweaks.

5. **Build a Culture of Curiosity:** Foster ongoing inquiry into your data—ensuring insights drive continuous growth, not just retrospective fascination.

19.2 Common Cognitive Biases in Data Interpretation

Bias Name	Description	Example in Time-Wealth Context	Mitigation Strategy
Confirmation Bias	Tendency to search for or interpret information that confirms pre-existing beliefs.	Focusing exclusively on days where TWS improved after caffeine, ignoring days it didn't.	Actively seek disconfirming evidence—compare high-TWS caffeine days with low-TWS caffeine days.
Recency Bias	Overweighting recent events when judging trends.	Believing your TWS is permanently high because the last three days were exceptional, ignoring earlier lows.	Use moving averages or look at 4-week trends rather than just the last week.
Availability Bias	Estimating likelihood based on how easily examples come to mind.	Assuming your afternoon slump only occurs on Wednesdays because that's when you recall feeling drained.	Review heatmaps of all weekdays to confirm slump patterns across the entire dataset.
Anchoring Bias	Relying too heavily on the first piece of information encountered.	Setting your TWS target to 30% because that was your Day 1 score, even if data suggests 40% is attainable.	Reassess targets periodically—use AI-recommended benchmarks based on peer data or historical extremes.
Survivorship Bias	Concentrating on "survivors" (successful experiments) while ignoring those that failed.	Celebrating only the leak-fix that halved LDR but forgetting two other fixes that had no effect.	Keep a log of all experiments, successful or not, to maintain a complete record of outcomes.
Overconfidence Bias	Overestimating one's ability to predict or control outcomes based on limited data.	Believing you can sustain 50% TWS indefinitely because you hit 50% for two days.	Simulate longer-term scenarios—use rolling 7-day charts and scenario analysis to temper expectations.

Surplus Detail Bias	Getting lost in granular data, missing the forest for the trees.	Obsessing over hourly LEM fluctuations while overlooking weekly TWS stagnation.	Begin analysis with high-level summaries (weekly or monthly), then drill down only when warranted by anomalies.
Clustering Illusion	Seeing patterns in random data, assuming non-existent trends.	Believing that every third day of the month is a slump day because you observed a few consecutive slumps.	Perform statistical tests (e.g., chi-square) or use AI to confirm pattern significance rather than eyeballing.

> **Mini-Lesson:** Recognizing and naming biases in your own thinking is the first step to neutralizing them. Keep a "Bias Log"—every time you suspect a skewed interpretation, annotate the bias and corrective action.

19.3 Building a Multi-Layered Interpretation Framework

A robust interpretation involves at least three layers of analysis:

1. **Descriptive Analysis:** What happened?
   - Example: "TWS dipped from 38% on Day 12 to 25% on Day 13."
   - Tools: Bar charts, line charts, tables summarizing raw values.
2. **Diagnostic Analysis:** Why did it happen?
   - Example: "Day 13 dip coincided with an unplanned 3-hour meeting and a broken ritual."
   - Tools: Overlay event annotations on charts, compare metric co-variations (scatter plots), review journal entries for qualitative context.
3. **Prescriptive Analysis:** What should I do next?
   - Example: "To prevent similar dips, schedule a recovery break before long meetings and automate meeting agendas to shorten duration by 15 minutes."
   - Tools: AI-generated suggestions, scenario modeling, A/B experiments.

By iterating through these layers—Describe, Diagnose, Prescribe—you ensure that data fuels purposeful evolution rather than random tinkering.

19.4 Descriptive Analysis Deep Dive

19.4.1 Trend Identification

- **Objective:** Detect overall trajectories—improving, declining, cyclical.
- **Technique:** Use line charts with moving averages; highlight periods of consistent upward or downward momentum.

Example: In your TWS line chart, overlay a 7-day and a 14-day moving average. If the 7-day crosses above the 14-day, it signals a recent positive momentum ("golden cross"); if it dips below, it indicates emerging decline.

- **Exercise:** Apply a 7-day and 14-day moving average to your TWS series. Mark each crossover date and note in your journal what interventions or disruptions coincided.

19.4.2 Inflection Point Detection

- **Objective:** Pinpoint dates where metrics change direction—peaks or troughs.
- **Technique:** Look for local maxima/minima in smoothed series or apply simple derivative approximations (difference between consecutive days).

Example: Use the "=SIGN(TWS_t – TWS_t–1)" formula in your spreadsheet to detect when the sign flips from positive to negative. Then, tag those dates for deeper diagnostic analysis.

- **Exercise:** Generate a column `TWS_Change` = `TWS_t - TWS_t-1`. Filter rows where `TWS_Change` changes sign from positive to negative (peak) or negative to positive (trough). List those dates for Day 19.5 diagnostic sessions.

19.4.3 Seasonal and Cyclical Patterns

- **Objective:** Uncover weekly, monthly, or quarterly cycles—recognizing that human energy and obligations often follow rhythms beyond daily fluctuations.
- **Technique:**

- **Weekday Averages:** Compute average TWS for each weekday over 30 days; use a bar chart to visualize.
- **Monthly Window:** If your 30-day span crosses a month boundary, compare first half vs. second half.
- **Quarter Comparisons:** If you have data from previous quarters (beyond 30 days), compare similar months.

Example: If Mondays consistently appear low and Fridays high, schedule low-stakes administrative tasks on Mondays and creative work on Fridays to leverage natural rhythms.

- **Exercise:** Create a bar chart of "Average TWS by Weekday" for your 30-day dataset. Then, annotate each bar with the exact numeric value. In your journal, propose block adjustments to align with these weekday patterns.

19.4.4 Distribution Analysis

- **Objective:** Understand the spread, central tendency, and skewness of metrics.
- **Technique:** Create histograms or box-and-whisker plots for daily values (e.g., RQS scores over 30 days).

Example: If your RQS distribution is heavily left-skewed (many low values), that indicates recovery quality is frequently subpar. Conversely, a right-skew suggests most breaks are highly restorative, with occasional poor exceptions.

- **Exercise:** Build a box-and-whisker plot of your daily RQS scores. Note the median, quartiles, and any outliers. Identify two outlier days and use diagnostic analysis (section 19.5) to explore their causes.

19.5 Diagnostic Analysis: Unpacking the "Why"

19.5.1 Overlaying Events on Time-Series Charts

- **Objective:** Link metric shifts to real-world events or interventions (e.g., tool changes, disruptions, new rituals).
- **Technique:** Use chart annotations or "vertical reference lines" to mark event dates.

Example: On your TWS line chart, add vertical lines for:

- Day 8: Block template overhaul.
- Day 15: AI automation launch.
- Day 22: Habit reinforcement intervention.

Visually, you can see if following those interventions, TWS rose, plateaued, or dipped.

- **Exercise:** Annotate your TWS line chart with at least five key events (from Weeks 1–4). For each annotation, write a one-sentence diagnostic note: "After AI agent launch on Day 18, TWS spiked by 5% over two days, likely due to improved scheduling."

19.5.2 Co-Variation and Correlation Analysis

- **Objective:** Quantify relationships between metrics to discover causal or predictive linkages.
- **Techniques:**
    1. **Scatter Plots with Regression:** As in Chapter 18, plot pairs (e.g., RQS vs. Next-Day TWS) to compute correlation coefficients (R^2).
    2. **Cross-Correlation Functions (CCF):** For time-series data, measure how one metric shifts relative to another over lags (e.g., does high RQS today correlate with high TWS two days later?).

Example: Use CCF to test whether high LDR on a given day predicts lower TWS three days later indicating that unaddressed leaks have delayed effects.

- **Exercise:** In Google Sheets or Python, calculate the Pearson correlation between daily LDR and TWS shifted by 1, 2, 3 days. Identify the lag with the highest negative correlation. Document your findings: "LDR on Day t correlates at –0.45 with TWS on Day t+2—suggesting we feel leak impact two days later."

19.5.3 Qualitative Contextualization via Journals

- **Objective:** Combine numerical analysis with narrative to unearth underlying causes that pure data cannot capture.

- **Technique:** For each significant metric anomaly (e.g., TWS drop below 20%), review corresponding journal entries:

    1. **Extract Qualitative Notes:** Copy one- to two-sentence reflections from your journal about that date (e.g., “Felt anxious due to impending presentation; skipped lunch-break ritual.”).

    2. **Identify Emotional or Environmental Triggers:** Note mood tags (□□●) and any described disruptions.

    3. **Synthesize Causes:** Document, in a table, metric anomaly, quantitative context, and qualitative insight.

Date	Metric Anomaly	Journal Note	Synthesis
2025-05-13	TWS dipped to 22% (local trough)	“Stressed about client meeting; skipped afternoon break; overslept”	Anxiety → Missed recovery → Late start → Lower TWS
2025-05-19	LDR spiked to 15%	“Phone left on desk; multiple Slack pings; no DND on”	Digital distractions due to lack of boundary enforcement → Elevated leak drag
2025-05-24	RQS dropped to 8/25, lowest of Week 4	“Had to handle family emergency; no time for break exercises”	Unexpected event → Forgone breaks → Poor recovery → Subsequent energy crash

- **Exercise:** For three most extreme anomalies (highest and lowest values) of any chosen metric, complete the table above. Then, brainstorm two micro-interventions to prevent similar scenarios (e.g., set stricter DND, plan contingency break rituals).

19.5.4 Scenario Analysis and “What If” Simulations

- **Objective:** Test how changes to one variable might cascade into others—helpful for planning experiments.

- **Technique:**
  - **Spreadsheet "What If" Tables:** Use data tables to simulate how reducing LDR by 5% might boost TWS, assuming a linear relationship (from your scatter analysis).
  - **AI-Assisted Scenario Planning:** Ask AI to model non-linear or complex interactions (e.g., "If I reduce LDR to 3% and improve RQS by 2 points, predict my TWS for the next 7 days, assuming current block adherence.").

Example:

1. In Sheets, create a table:
   - Column A: Hypothetical LDR values (2%, 4%, 6%, 8%).
   - Column B: Predicted TWS = 50% – (LDR × 2). (Assuming each 1% of LDR reduces TWS by 2% based on past regression).
2. Observe that at LDR = 2%, TWS = 46%; LDR = 4%, TWS = 42%, etc.

Exercise: Build a "What If" table for LDR and TWS using your own regression formula (from section 19.5.2). Then, ask an AI:

pgsql
CopyEdit
```
"Given LDR values ranging from 2% to 10%, and assuming each 1% LDR
change equates to a 1.8% TWS change, generate a seven-day TWS forecast
where LDR is held constant at 3%."
```

- Compare AI output to your spreadsheet results and note any differences or new insights.

19.6 Prescriptive Analysis: From Insights to Interventions

19.6.1 Prioritizing Interventions via Impact/Effort Matrix

- **Objective:** Decide which insights to act on first, balancing potential impact against required effort.

- **Technique:** Create a 2×2 matrix:

	High Effort	Low Effort
High Impact	Strategic Projects (e.g., full block redesign)	Quick Wins (e.g., adjust break timing)
Low Impact	Nice-to-Have (e.g., redesign dashboard aesthetics)	Do Later (e.g., refine rare rituals)

- **Example:**
  - **Insight:** LDR spikes mid-week are huge drains → **High Impact**, **Low Effort**: Enforce "Midweek Digital Sabbath" block.
  - **Insight:** Subtle correlation between room lighting and RQS → **Low Impact**, **High Effort**: Install new smart lights.
- **Exercise:** List five diagnostic insights from days 1–28. For each, estimate impact (High/Low) and effort (High/Low). Populate your Impact/Effort Matrix and highlight two "High Impact/Low Effort" interventions to implement next.

19.6.2 Crafting SMART Experiments

- **Objective:** Design experiments that are Specific, Measurable, Achievable, Relevant, and Time-Bound.

Technique: Use a simple template:

vbnet
CopyEdit
```
Experiment Name: "Midweek Digital Sabbath Trial"
Specific: Block Wednesday 1–4 PM as device-free work, enforcing DND.
Measurable: Measure LDR (%) and TWS (%) on Wednesdays for two weeks
versus baseline.
Achievable: Only requires adjusting calendar and auto-replies; team
informed.
```

```
Relevant: Aims to reduce midweek LDR spikes identified in heatmap.
Time-Bound: Pilot for two consecutive Wednesdays (Dates: 2025-06-04
and 2025-06-11).
```

-
- **Exercise:** Translate your two High Impact/Low Effort interventions into SMART experiments. Schedule them in your calendar and set reminders for data capture and review.

19.6.3 Crafting AI-Powered Action Plans

- **Objective:** Leverage AI as a continuous consultant to translate diagnoses into concrete to-dos.
- **Technique:** Provide AI with structured prompts containing insights and ask for actionable plans.

Example Prompt:

pgsql
CopyEdit

```
"I observed that my LDR averages 10% on Mondays, and my TWS dips to
20% on Tuesdays. Suggest a week-long action plan with daily steps to
reduce Monday LDR by at least 3% and boost Tuesday TWS by 5%. Include
both behavioral changes and AI automations."
```

AI might respond with:

1. **Behavioral:** Move weekly team meeting from Monday to Tuesday to reduce meeting drift.
2. **Automation:** Set up a Zap to summarize Monday's email batches at 3 PM, preventing inbox drag.
3. **Ritual:** Introduce a "Monday Morning 5-Minute Stretch" micro-ritual to combat early-week inertia.

- **Exercise:** Craft two AI prompts—one focused on midweek improvements and one on optimizing weekends. Record AI's suggestions and plan to test at least three of them over the next week.

19.6.4 Iterative A/B Testing of Interventions

- **Objective:** Rigorously compare the effectiveness of two variants to isolate the superior one.
- **Technique:**
    1. **Define Variables:** Choose one change to test—e.g., "Break Protocol A: 10-min walk" vs. "Break Protocol B: 5-min meditation + 5-min stretch."
    2. **Randomize or Alternate Days:** Assign Protocol A to odd dates and Protocol B to even dates over a 10-day span.
    3. **Measure Outcome:** Compare RQS and FBR on those days; compute average scores for A vs. B.
    4. **Statistical Check:** Use a t-test (if sample size sufficient) or compare means to declare a "winner."

Example:

- Protocol A mean RQS = 18.2; Protocol B mean RQS = 16.4.
- Interpretation: Protocol A outperforms; adopt 10-min walk as default.
- **Exercise:** Identify one area where you have two plausible interventions (e.g., two micro-ritual variants). Conduct an A/B test over the next 10 days. Document methodology, record results, and decide which protocol to adopt permanently.

19.7 Advanced Techniques: Predictive & Prescriptive Modeling

19.7.1 Building a Simple Predictive Model

- **Objective:** Use machine learning to forecast key metrics based on historical data, guiding proactive adjustments.
- **Technique:**
    1. **Collect Data:** Compile a dataset with daily features—TWS, LDR, RQS, BCR, day of week, blocks adhered, number of AI interactions.

2. **Choose a Model:** For simplicity, use linear regression or decision tree (no-code tools: Google AutoML, Airtable Blocks, or Excel's "Data Analysis" add-in).
3. **Train & Validate:** Split data into training (Days 1–20) and testing (Days 21–30). Evaluate RMSE or accuracy.
4. **Deploy:** Use the model to predict Day 31 TWS; compare to actual Day 31 (when you collect new data).

Example: If your model predicts Day 31 TWS will be 35% but actual is 30%, analyze feature residuals to see which inputs (e.g., unexpectedly low RQS) most contributed to the error.

- **Exercise:**
  1. Export Days 1–30 metrics to AutoML Tables or Excel.
  2. Train a simple regression model predicting TWS from LDR, RQS, and day of week.
  3. Document model coefficients: which feature has highest impact?
  4. Use the model to predict TWS for the next week and plan one intervention if predicted TWS falls below 30%.

19.7.2 Prescriptive Analytics with AI Agents

- **Objective:** Move from prediction to prescription—ask AI not just what might happen, but what to do about it.
- **Technique:**

Provide AI with current data snapshot and ask for prioritized action list:

matlab
CopyEdit
```
"Using my current metrics—TWS 28%, LDR 12%, RQS 14, BCR 82%, UCR 90%—recommend the top three actionable changes I should implement in the next 48 hours to push TWS above 35%."
```

○

    - AI may suggest automating leak interventions, refining recovery protocols, or adding micro-ritual for midday peaks.

Exercise: At the start of Week 6, ask your AI:

pgsql
CopyEdit
```
"Given the first 35 days of my data, propose a 5-day tactical sprint to elevate my TWS by at least 5%. Include both behavior and system-level recommendations."
```

- Test at least two suggestions; measure impact against control.

19.7.3 Incorporating Anomaly Detection

- **Objective:** Automatically flag metric anomalies—unexpected spikes or drops—so you can diagnose them promptly.
- **Technique:**
    1. Use AI or built-in tools:
        - **Google Data Studio:** Enable the "Anomaly Detection" feature on time-series charts—outliers are highlighted.

Python (optional): Implement z-score detection:

python
CopyEdit
```python
import pandas as pd
from scipy import stats

df = pd.read_csv('metrics.csv', parse_dates=['Date'])
df['TWS_z'] = stats.zscore(df['TWS_%'])
anomalies = df[abs(df['TWS_z']) > 2]  # |z| > 2
```

-
- **No-Code Platforms:** Services like BigML or DataRobot provide auto anomaly detection for uploaded datasets.

- **Exercise:**
    1. In Google Data Studio, enable anomaly detection on your TWS line chart.
    2. Identify all anomalies (|z| > 2) over 30 days.
    3. For each flagged anomaly, perform diagnostic analysis (section 19.5) and record findings in a dedicated "Anomalies" journal section.

19.8 Case Study: From Data to Lifelong Transformation

Background: Jordan, a marketing consultant, completed the 30-day Time-Wealth sprint. Initial metrics:

- TWS: 18% → 28% by Day 30.
- LDR: 12% → 6%.
- RQS: 10 → 18.

Despite improvements, Jordan felt plateauing—TWS hovered around 28% for Days 25–30. To break through, Jordan:

1. **Descriptive Review (Day 31):**
    - TWS moving average showed plateau from Day 24 onward.
    - Weekly average LDR was 6%, but BCR dipped to 75% on Tuesday/Thursday.
2. **Diagnostic Deep Dive:**
    - **Heatmap Analysis:** Revealed Tuesday afternoons (2–4 PM) had LEM < 3%.
    - **Journal Context:** Day 26 note: "Scheduled client calls over lunch; skipped break rituals."
    - **Scatter Analysis:** Poor RQS (<15) on Monday predicted low TWS on Tuesday.

3. **Prescriptive Planning:**
    - **Impact/Effort Matrix:**
        - **High Impact/Low Effort:** Introduce "Pre-Tuesday Ritual" at 12 PM to safeguard breaks before afternoon calls.
        - **High Impact/High Effort:** Reschedule recurring Tuesday client calls to Monday or Friday when possible.

SMART Experiment:

vbnet
CopyEdit
```
Experiment: "Tuesday Lunch Break Protection"
Specific: From next Tuesday onward, schedule a 12–12:30 PM Break Block
with DND, regardless of call load.
Measurable: Track RQS and LEM on Tuesdays for the next two weeks vs.
baseline.
Achievable: Only requires calendar adjustment; clients informed.
Relevant: Aims to improve midweek focus dips.
Time-Bound: Pilot for four consecutive Tuesdays.
```

-
- **AI-Prescribed Tactic:**

Prompt:

mathematica
CopyEdit
```
"Recommend three AI automations to enforce Tuesday Break Block and
reduce late-afternoon LDR."
```

-
- AI suggestions:
    - Auto-respond on Slack during 12–12:30 PM with "In Focus Break – will reply at 12:30."
    - Mute email notifications via Zapier during the block.

        - Generate a calendar reminder with "Break Now!" message on phone.

4. **Implementation & Outcomes (Days 32–39):**
    - **RQS Tuesday:** Improved from 14 to 20 average.
    - **LEM (2–4 PM Tuesdays):** Rose from 3% to 7%.
    - **TWS Next Day (Wednesdays):** Increased from 26% to 32%.
    - **BCR Tuesday:** Climbing from 75% to 90% as protected break prevented overruns.
5. **Meta-Reflection:**

    "By layering descriptive, diagnostic, and prescriptive analysis, I transformed a stubborn plateau into a new growth trajectory. The Tuesday Break Block experiment exemplified how a single insight, properly executed, can cascade into higher presence, better recovery, and smoother cycles."

Key Takeaway: Lifelong growth emerges when you treat data not as historical records, but as living signals guiding continuous, precise interventions.

19.9 Advanced Exercises for Mastery

19.9.1 Multi-Metric Cohort Analysis

- **Objective:** Compare your metrics against a cohort—team members, accountability partners, or professionals in your field.
- **Technique:**
    1. **Data Collection:** Aggregate anonymized metrics from 3–5 peers over the same 30-day period.
    2. **Cohort Visualization:** Create side-by-side box plots or overlaid line charts for TWS, LDR, and RQS.

3. **Benchmarking:** Identify where you rank—top quartile, middle half, or bottom quartile.
4. **Action Steps:** If in the lower quartile for any metric, designate a "Benchmark Improvement Sprint" targeting that metric for the next 15 days.

- **Exercise:** Coordinate with two teammates to share aggregated metrics (e.g., weekly LDR). Build cohort box plots in Google Sheets. Discuss results in Peer Pod and set collective improvement goals.

19.9.2 Sentiment-Linked Metric Interpretation

- **Objective:** Explore how emotional state influences metrics and vice versa.
- **Technique:**

Extract Sentiment Scores: From journal entries, use AI to assign a sentiment score (1 = very negative, 5 = very positive) for each day's top insight.

pgsql
CopyEdit
```
"Rate the sentiment of this text on a scale of 1–5: [insert journal insight]."
```

  -
  - **Merge Sentiment with Metrics:** Add a `Sentiment_Score` column to `DailyMetrics`.
  - **Scatter Plot:** Plot `Sentiment_Score` (X-axis) vs. `TWS_%` (Y-axis). Add trendline.
  - **Heatmap:** Create a 7-day sentiment heatmap similar to LEM heatmap—Days vs. Sentiment Score.

- **Interpretation:**
  - Positive correlation suggests emotional well-being fuels presence.
  - Discrepancies (high sentiment but low TWS) indicate possible superficial positivity masking productivity dips.

- **Exercise:** Conduct sentiment analysis on your last 30 journal insights. Create the scatter plot and heatmap. In your journal, reflect on any disconnects and propose two emotional well-being experiments (e.g., gratitude journaling, midweek social check-ins) for the next week.

19.9.3 Longitudinal Scenario Planning

- **Objective:** Use your 30-day insights to project and adapt over a year, accounting for seasonal shifts and life events.
- **Technique:**
    1. **Seasonal Anchors:** Identify recurring annual events—Q4 holidays, Q2 busy quarters, etc.
    2. **Extend Metrics:** Simulate your monthly LDR, TWS, and RQS values for 12 months by applying average monthly deltas from your 30-day data.
        - If TWS improved by 10% over one month, project similar monthly gains, then taper to realistic 2–3% growth per month.
    3. **Risk Scenarios:** Add hypothetical disruptions—business travel, family events—modeling their impact as metric dips.
        - For each disruption, simulate a 5% TWS drop and 3% LDR spike for the affected week.
    4. **Adaptive Interventions:** Define contingent rituals:
        - Business trip → "Travel Recovery Protocol" (Day before departure: pack ritual kit; during trip: schedule ultradian breaks in hotel).
        - Family holiday → "Family Connect Ritual" (use digital sabbath to maximize presence).
- **Exercise:** In your spreadsheet, create a "Yearly Projection" table with 12 rows (months) and columns for projected TWS, LDR, RQS. Start with April 2025 values, then apply a 2% monthly TWS gain and 1% LDR reduction, incorporating three hypothetical disruptions (June conference, September move, December holidays). Use the table to plan quarterly rituals that counteract these dips.

19.10 Ritual: The Monthly “Data Deep Dive”

19.10.1 Ritual Components

- **Duration:** 90 minutes scheduled on the first Saturday of each month.
- **Environment:** Quiet space with large screen to view dashboards, printed reports, and journal.
- **Materials:**
    - Master Dashboard printouts or live links.
    - Journal entries from the past month.
    - Colored pens (blue, green, red) for annotations.
    - Sticky notes or index cards for action items.

19.10.2 Step-by-Step Ritual

1. **Centering Moment (2 min):** Three deep breaths, reciting your updated Time-Wealth Manifesto.
2. **High-Level Scan (10 min):** Review monthly aggregates for TWS, LDR, BCR, RQS. Note “Star Metrics” (those meeting or exceeding targets) and “Risk Metrics” (those below thresholds).
3. **Trend Analysis (25 min):**
    - Examine the TWS growth curve; mark any new plateaus or accelerations.
    - Review heatmap for hourly LEM—identify new focus windows or emerging slump periods.
    - Use a colored pen to circle significant inflection points and write a one-word label (e.g., “New client trial,” “Vacation week”).
4. **Cohort & Benchmark Check (10 min):** If available, compare your metrics to a cohort or historical data from the same month last year. Highlight where you lead or lag peers.

5. **Qualitative Review (15 min):** Read journal insights—one per week. For each:
    - Summarize the key lesson in a 10-word sentence.
    - Annotate the corresponding date on the dashboard with a sticky note (e.g., "Week 2: midweek slump fix").
6. **Prescriptive Mapping (20 min):**
    - Use sticky notes to list "Wins," "Challenges," and "Opportunities" on a large sheet labeled "Monthly SWOT for Time-Wealth."
    - For each "Challenge," propose one experiment or intervention for the next month.
    - For each "Opportunity," schedule an AI prompt or calendar block to explore further.
7. **Action Planning (8 min):** Translate top 3 items from the "Opportunities" column into SMART goals. Post on an index card and place on your desk for daily visibility.
8. **Closure (5 min):** Express gratitude for your progress—write a one-sentence "Thank You" note to yourself in your journal. Recite aloud:

"I honor my time-wealth journey and commit to continuous learning."

Exercise: Schedule your first "Monthly Data Deep Dive" for the first Saturday after finishing Chapter 19. Gather all materials and follow the above steps. Document any immediate "Aha!" moments in your journal.

19.11 AI Prompts for Continuing Insight Generation

Use AI to sustain interpretation and uncover deeper patterns beyond manual review:

Monthly Neural Network Check-In:

perl
CopyEdit
```
"Review my last 30-day data and journal entries. Generate a 300-word
```

```
executive summary highlighting emerging patterns, emotional insights, and three recommendations for next month's experiments."
```

- **Bias Detection Partner:**

typescript
CopyEdit
```
"Evaluate my interpretation notes from this month. Identify any potential cognitive biases at play and suggest ways to re-examine conclusions objectively."
```

- **Narrative Storyboard Creator:**

vbnet
CopyEdit
```
"Craft a short narrative storyboard (6–8 slides worth) that tells the story of my Time-Wealth evolution over the past four weeks, focusing on key inflection points."
```

- **"Hypothesis Generator" Prompt:**

css
CopyEdit
```
"Given the correlation matrix of my metrics, propose two hypotheses about cause-effect relationships. For each, recommend a simple experiment to test it."
```

- **"Devil's Advocate" Prompt:**

perl
CopyEdit
```
"Challenge my assumption that automating my email triage is the best next step. Provide two counterarguments and two alternative focus areas."
```

-

Tip: Store all AI outputs in a dedicated "Insight Library" section of your journal or knowledge base to revisit as you accumulate more data.

19.12 Case Study: Sustaining Growth Beyond 30 Days

Background: Patrice, a UX researcher, completed the initial 30-day Time-Wealth sprint. By Day 30:

- TWS: 40%
- LDR: 3%
- BCR: 92%
- RQS: 21

Despite these robust metrics, Patrice feared regression once daily support slowed. Over the next three months, Patrice applied Chapter 19 frameworks to remain in growth mode.

1. **Monthly Deep Dives:**
    - During Month 2, Patrice discovered that TWS dipped every second Friday (data revealed a recurring "deadline anxiety" lead-in).
    - Response: Scheduled a "Pre-Deadline Ritual"—a 10-minute visualization session preceding those Fridays. TWS stabilized above 38% thereafter.
2. **Bias Mitigation Exercises:**
    - Patrice's "Bias Log" flagged several occurrences of recency bias—overweighting positive results from recent client wins and underestimating ensuing time drains.
    - To counteract, paired Mondays with "Critical Reflection" sessions, wherein Patrice reviewed not only wins but also potential blind spots.
3. **Cohort Accountability:**
    - Joined a broader "Time-Wealth Collective" (10 professionals) sharing monthly metrics. An aggregated radar chart revealed Patrice lagged peers in "Digital Boundary Consistency."

- Intervention: Adopted two peers' "Evening Lockout Protocol" (phones off at 8 PM). Consequently, RQS on weekends spiked by 15%, and Monday TWS increased from 32% to 36%.

4. **Continuous Learning Loops:**
    - Each month, Patrice read one academic paper on productivity neuroscience or digital minimalism, then tested one extractable tactic (e.g., "80/20 task prioritization" from new research).
    - On Month 3, implemented a "Weekly Digital Sabbath" (6 hours every Saturday), which further reduced average LDR from 3% to 2% by Month 4.
5. **Long-Term Vision Alignment:**
    - In the annual review, Patrice aligned Time-Wealth metrics with broader life goals: improved work–life balance, creative side-project time, and mental health resilience.
    - Established a "Year-Two Roadmap" with targeted TWS goals for each quarter (e.g., Q1: ≥42%, Q2: ≥44%, Q3: ≥46%, Q4: ≥48%).

Patrice's Reflection:
"Data interpretation isn't a one-off task—it's a lifelong habit. By cycling through descriptive, diagnostic, and prescriptive layers each month, I turned the initial sprint into a sustainable cadence. Three months in, my system feels second nature, and my metrics validate that growth can persist even when life throws curveballs."

19.13 Common Pitfalls & Best Practices in Interpretation

Pitfall	Best Practice
Disregarding Qualitative Context	Always pair quantitative charts with at least one journal reflection or anecdote.
Overfitting to Short-Term Fluctuations	Prioritize weekly or monthly aggregates—treat daily anomalies as signals to investigate, not as sole decision triggers.

Anchoring on Early Data Points	Periodically reset baselines; do not let early low or high values constrain future targets.
Failing to Validate Hypotheses	After diagnosing a cause, always test via controlled experiments before assuming causality.
Ignoring Non-Metric Success Indicators	Incorporate qualitative feedback—client praise, team morale, personal well-being—into your interpretation framework.
Cherry-Picking Data to Confirm Narratives	Use full datasets and statistical methods—avoid selecting only data that aligns with your story.
Misreading Correlation as Causation	When two metrics move together, dive deeper with diagnostic tools (journal context, CCF) before declaring one "caused" the other.
Overloading Dashboards with Annotations	Limit annotations to top 3–5 per chart; for deeper notes, link to a separate "Insights" document rather than crowding visuals.
Not Revisiting Past Interpretations	Schedule a "Quarterly Interpretation Audit" to reassess whether past conclusions still hold in light of new data.
Applying One-Size-Fits-All Solutions	Tailor interventions to your unique rhythms and context; what works for a peer may not work for you without adaptation.

19.14 Ritual: The Daily "Insight Capture" Bookmark

Fuel ongoing interpretation by capturing immediate observations:

1. **Trigger (Morning Review):**
    - When you open your dashboard each morning, pause 2–3 minutes to jot the first insight that jumps out—e.g., "TWS dipped yesterday; check LDR to see if new leaks emerged."
2. **Midday Check-In (Optional, 1 min):**

- Briefly scan your real-time metrics (live dashboard). If you notice an anomaly (e.g., sudden LDR spike), note it immediately—no judgment, just record.

3. **Evening Wrap-Up (3–5 min):**
    - Post all chart-based experiments or observations into a dedicated "Insight Capture" section of your journal. Categorize each as "Descriptive," "Diagnostic," or "Prescriptive."
4. **Weekly Synthesis (Part of Chapter 18 Ritual):**
    - Review the week's "Insight Capture" entries and distill them into 1–2 sentences for each week.

Tip: Use voice-to-text on your phone to capture midday or evening insights on the fly—minimize friction to encourage consistent practice.

19.15 Integrating Interpretation into Your Infinite Cycles

Your Infinite Cycle phases (Ch. 2) become richer when imbued with ongoing interpretation:

1. **Intention Setting:**
    - **Before Cycle Start:** Review yesterday's "Insight Capture" to prime your intention—e.g., "Today, I focus on minimizing LDR during my 2 PM block."
2. **Focused Action:**
    - **Mid-Cycle:** Keep a small "Insight Capture" widget or note open to jot quick observations—e.g., "Feeling distracted by Slack pings; consider adjusting DND mid-block."
3. **Immediate Feedback:**
    - **Post-Block Chart Review:** Examine block-specific metrics (LEM, RQS) for that session. Write a short diagnostic note: "LEM=8% (↑2%); RQS=19 (↓1)"
4. **Renewal & Adjustment:**

- **Update Next Block Plan:** Based on immediate feedback, decide: “For next cycle, I will add a 2-minute micro-ritual to close Slack.”

By weaving interpretation into each cycle, you ensure that every metric informs your next intention—enabling true continuous improvement.

19.16 Reflection & Preview of Chapter 20

You have now:

- Mastered cognitive biases and how they can mislead interpretation.
- Built a multi-layered framework—descriptive, diagnostic, prescriptive—for analyzing your data.
- Performed trend identification, inflection point detection, seasonal analysis, and distribution studies.
- Conducted overlay exercises to link real-world events with metric shifts.
- Executed scenario planning and A/B testing to validate causal inferences.
- Leveraged advanced predictive and prescriptive analytics—including simple ML and AI agent prompts—to forecast and act.
- Developed rituals—Monthly Deep Dives and Daily Insight Capture—to institutionalize interpretation.
- Completed case studies demonstrating how interpretation drives lifelong growth.

Next chapter: In **Chapter 20: Cultivating a Time-Wealth Mindset**, you'll explore the psychological underpinnings that sustain high performance—beliefs, values, mental models, and self-talk. You will learn how to nurture resilience, abundance thinking, and a growth mindset so that your system not only functions mechanically but thrives through challenges, setbacks, and evolving aspirations.

Journal Prompt:

1. *“Which interpretive framework resonated most deeply with me today, and why?”*

2. *“How will I integrate Monthly Deep Dives into my long-term routine?”*
3. *“What mental model will I adopt to guard against confirmation bias in my next data review?”*

By answering these, you ensure that data interpretation remains not merely a task but a mindset—fueling your infinite cycle of learning, growth, and time-wealth.

- Reschedule affected blocks into floating slots; note time taken to realign (target < 10 min).

2. **Emotional Resilience Inventory:** Each week, list one emotional challenge (stress, frustration) and one behavioral response (overworking, avoidance). For each:
    - Identify a resilience skill to deploy (mindful breathing, reaching out for support).
    - Track how deploying that skill affects your next-day metrics (e.g., if journaling reduces Monday LDR by 2%).
3. **Ready-To-Go Rituals:** Create a “Resilience Kit” with pre-selected micro-rituals for acute stress—e.g., a 1-minute grounding exercise, a 5-minute gratitude practice, and a “Text a Friend” script for social support. Keep this Kit visible (a post-it on your monitor or a folder in your journaling app).

Exercise: Over the next month, whenever a real disruption occurs—travel, illness, unexpected demand—explicitly choose a “Resilience-Kit Ritual” and log how quickly and effectively you bounce back (measured by time to regain a target LEM or TWS).

20.13 Gratitude and Positive Psychology Practices to Reinforce Mindset

Gratitude isn’t just feel-good fluff; research shows that regular gratitude practices increase resilience, improve cognitive function, and reduce perceived stress. In a Time-Wealth context, gratitude shifts focus from “What went wrong?” to “What’s going right?”—fueling abundance and motivation.

20.13.1 Daily Gratitude Ritual

- **Timing:** At either morning primer or evening wrap-up.
- **Format:** Write three specific, time-related gratitudes—e.g.,
    1. "I'm grateful I had an uninterrupted 90-min Deep Work block today."
    2. "I appreciate that my Break Protocol recharged me when I felt a slump."
    3. "I'm thankful for my AI agent's timely reminder that allowed me to finish a task early."
- **Technique:** Use bullet points, keep to no more than two sentences each.

Mini-Lesson: Specificity matters—"I'm grateful for my calendar block" is less impactful than "I'm grateful that my 10 AM block was uninterrupted, letting me finish the client deck."

20.13.2 Positivity Ratios and Emotional Granularity

- **Positivity Ratio:** The ratio of positive (gratitude, pride, joy) to negative (frustration, guilt, fear) emotional expressions. Research suggests sustaining a ratio of at least **3:1** fosters flourishing.
- **Emotional Granularity:** Instead of labeling feelings simply "good" or "bad," use nuanced terms—"I felt content" vs. "I felt anxious." Higher granularity improves emotion regulation.

Exercise: For three days, rate your dominant emotions in each block using a 5-point scale (1 = very negative, 3 = neutral, 5 = very positive). Compute your daily Positivity Ratio (# of positive blocks ÷ # of negative blocks). Aim to increase this ratio over time by introducing gratitude and mindful breaks.

20.13.3 Strengths-Based Journaling

- **Objective:** Identify and leverage personal strengths—creativity, persistence, empathy—in service of time-wealth.
- **Technique:**

1. **Strengths Discovery:** Use a standard strengths inventory (VIA Survey, StrengthsFinder) or ask peers for three strengths they see in you.
2. **Strengths Application Planning:** For each of your top 5 strengths, write one way to deploy it in your time-wealth system—e.g.:
   - Creativity → Design novel micro-rituals.
   - Perseverance → Sustain daily journaling even when busy.
   - Empathy → Build social feedback loops in your Peer Pod.
3. **Weekly Reflection:** Document one instance per week where you applied a strength and the resulting positive effect on your metrics or mindset.

Exercise: Conduct a "Strengths Inventory." Identify your top three strengths and, in your journal, list one concrete way to use each strength to overcome a time-wealth challenge you face (e.g., improving boundary enforcement).

20.14 Ritual: The Daily Mindset Check-In

A micro-ritual dedicated solely to your inner narrative ensures that mindset remains top of mind, not an afterthought.

20.14.1 Components of the Check-In (Duration: 90 seconds)

1. **Pause & Breathe (10s):** Close your eyes; inhale deeply for 4 seconds, exhale for 6.
2. **Self-Talk Scan (20s):** Mentally review any dominant thoughts about time since the last check—label them as "Scarcity," "Growth," or "Neutral."
3. **Values Alignment Query (20s):** Ask: "Did my last block align with my top value of [e.g., Connection]?" If not, plan a compensatory break to honor that value.
4. **Affirmation Recital (20s):** Speak your most relevant affirmation aloud—e.g., "Moment by moment, I craft abundance."
5. **Future Intention (20s):** Set a specific micro-intention for the next 60 minutes—such as "In the next hour, I will complete my block with focused presence and conclude with a

gratitude note."

Tip: Attach this Check-In to a habitual anchor—immediately after your calibration breath for blocks (Chapter 8 Rituals), or at the top of each hour via a timer.

20.14.2 Tracking Your Check-Ins

- **Self-Report Table:** In your daily journal, create a small table with columns:
  - Block Start Time
  - Dominant Thought Label (S/G/N)
  - Value Alignment? (Y/N)
  - Affirmation Used
  - Next Micro-Intention

Example:

Block Time	Thought Label	Value Aligned?	Affirmation	Next Intention
10:00 AM	Scarcity	N	"I create space for breakthroughs."	"I will set a timer for a 5-min break."
11:10 AM	Growth	Y	"Learning fuels my momentum."	"I will focus fully on client deck."
2:30 PM	Neutral	Y	"Presence is power."	"I will take a 2-min stretch break."

- **Analysis:** At day's end, tally how many blocks began with "Scarcity" vs. "Growth" thoughts and how often values were aligned. Compute a **Mindset Alignment Ratio (MAR)** = (Growth-aligned blocks ÷ Total Blocks) × 100. Aim to ratchet MAR upward week by week.

Exercise: For one full day, perform the Mindset Check-In before every block. At the next day's evening journal, calculate your MAR and reflect on any patterns—e.g., "My early-morning blocks often begin with scarcity thoughts; I need a stronger morning ritual."

20.15 AI Prompts for Continuous Mindset Coaching

Leverage AI as a personalized coach to challenge biases and reinforce growth:

Bias Identification:

swift
CopyEdit
```
"Here are five recent negative self-talk scripts I recorded. Identify any cognitive biases at work and suggest reframes for each."
```

1.

Values Alignment Check:

pgsql
CopyEdit
```
"Given my top values of Connection, Creativity, and Growth, propose three daily micro-actions I can take to honor each value this week."
```

2.

Mental Model Reinforcement:

pgsql
CopyEdit
```
"Explain how the concept of 'Margin of Safety' applies to scheduling my blocks and suggest two ways I can build more time buffers into my calendar."
```

3.

Resilience Coaching:

less
CopyEdit
```
"I'm facing a setback: my LDR spiked to 12% yesterday. Coach me
```

```
through a 5-minute resilience routine to recover my focus and renew my commitment."
```

4.

Affirmation Refresh:

php
CopyEdit
```
"Generate five new affirmations to counteract the thought 'I'll never catch up.' Use growth-focused, present-tense language."
```

5.

> **Tip:** Save AI outputs in a "Mindset Playbook" section of your journal. Periodically review and refresh these prompts to keep the content dynamic and personally resonant.

20.16 Common Pitfalls in Mindset Cultivation & Proactive Fixes

Pitfall	Fix
Treating Mindset as "Optional"	Integrate Mindset Check-In ritual into every block; treat like any other non-negotiable part of your system.
Overemphasizing Metrics Over Mindset	Balance weekly chart reviews with weekly mindset reviews—schedule both equally.
Surface-Level Affirmations Without Depth	Pair affirmations with deeper exercises (visualization, journaling) to root them in personal meaning.
Ignoring Subtle Self-Talk Patterns	Use the "Self-Talk Log" consistently; review entries weekly to catch recurring negative themes.
Neglecting Values Alignment	Revisit values exercise monthly—values evolve; ensure your system adapts as your priorities shift.
Cognitive Dissonance (Say vs. Do Gap)	If you're reciting affirmations but not acting on them, identify practical steps to align behavior with language.

Underestimating Emotional Impact	Use sentiment analysis (AI prompts) to quantify mood swings; adjust recovery practices when negativity rises.
Resilience Rituals Forgotten Under Stress	Pre-schedule "Disruption Drills" monthly and keep a visible checklist to ensure they're executed.
Relying on Willpower Alone	Build environmental and social scaffolds (Peer Pod, accountability partners) to support mindset when willpower wanes.

Mini-Lesson: Mindset cultivation is not a one-time action—it's an ongoing series of micro-commitments reinforced by rituals, social support, and periodic recalibration.

20.17 Integrating Mindset into Your Infinite Cycles

Mindset seamlessly weaves into every phase of your Infinite Cycle (Chapter 2):

1. **Intention Setting:**
    - Anchor intentions in growth-oriented beliefs—e.g., "Today, I welcome any data insights as feedback rather than judgement."
    - Use your Daily Mindset Check-In to prime that intention before launching a block.
2. **Focused Action:**
    - When executing a block, maintain a "Growth vs. Fixed" awareness—note if you catch yourself slipping into a limiting narrative; gently reset to an empowering affirmation.
3. **Immediate Feedback:**
    - As you review block metrics (LEM, RQS), consciously frame them as data points rather than personal judgments.
    - Use self-talk prompts: "Metric X shows an opportunity to improve; I embrace the challenge."
4. **Renewal & Adjustment:**

- When deciding next steps, inject abundance thinking—e.g., “I have plenty of time to iterate this ritual until it works.”
- Refer to mental models like Compound Interest—“Even small daily tweaks compound, so I will persist.”

Insight: Mindset is the emotional-cognitive substrate that turns raw data and structured practices into an evolving, self-correcting system—where each cycle reinforces both skill and belief.

20.18 Reflection & Next Steps Beyond Chapter 20

You have now:

- Explored growth versus fixed mindsets and recognized scarcity/abundance thinking.
- Learned cognitive restructuring to reframe limiting beliefs.
- Identified core values and aligned them with your time investments.
- Adopted mental models that clarify complex time-wealth concepts.
- Cultivated empowering self-talk through systematic journaling and affirmations.
- Practiced visualization and future-self exercises to anchor long-term motivation.
- Studied a case example demonstrating how mindset work catalyzes metric breakthroughs.
- Built resilience skills, gratitude rituals, and positive psychology practices.
- Established the Daily Mindset Check-In and Monthly Deep Dive rituals to institutionalize mindset.
- Used AI prompts to continuously reinforce and refine mindset.
- Integrated mindset cultivation into every phase of your Infinite Cycle.

Looking ahead: The chapters to come will explore the social and collaborative dimensions of Time-Wealth—delving into how teams, organizations, and communities can co-create time-wealth ecosystems. You will learn to design group cycles, collective dashboards, and shared

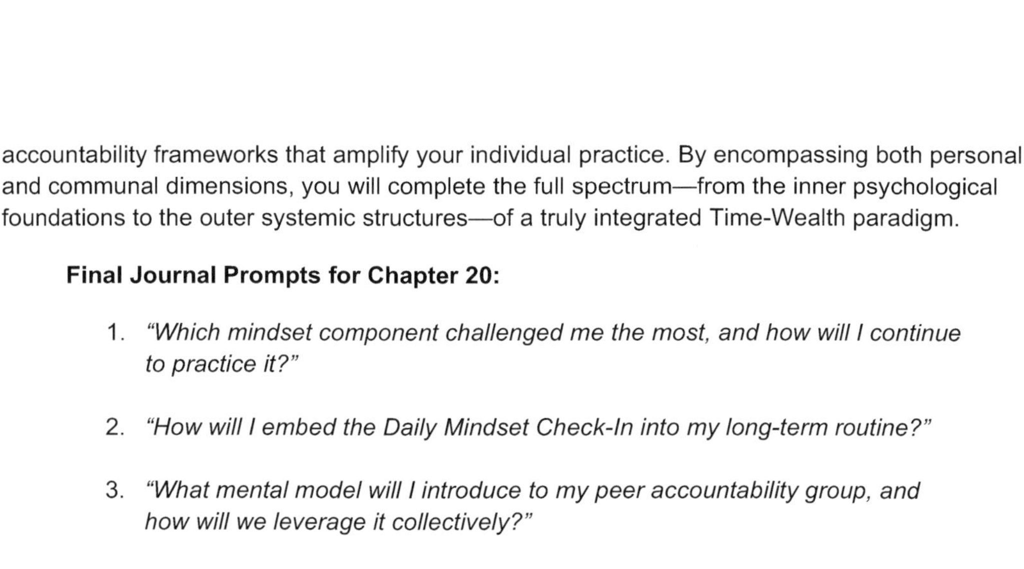

accountability frameworks that amplify your individual practice. By encompassing both personal and communal dimensions, you will complete the full spectrum—from the inner psychological foundations to the outer systemic structures—of a truly integrated Time-Wealth paradigm.

Final Journal Prompts for Chapter 20:

1. *"Which mindset component challenged me the most, and how will I continue to practice it?"*
2. *"How will I embed the Daily Mindset Check-In into my long-term routine?"*
3. *"What mental model will I introduce to my peer accountability group, and how will we leverage it collectively?"*

By answering these, you solidify Chapter 20's lessons and prepare to extend your practice beyond the self—building time-wealth cultures that ripple outward.

Made in the USA
Columbia, SC
16 June 2025